INDIRA GANDHI

THE STORY OF A LEADER

SHAHANA DASGUPTA

RUPA

For Ma and Baba

Published by
Rupa Publications India Pvt. Ltd 2004]
7/16, Ansari Road, Daryaganj
New Delhi 110002

Sales centres:
Allahabad Bengaluru Chennai
Hyderabad Jaipur Kathmandu
Kolkata Mumbai

Photographs courtesy: Nehru Memorial Museum, PIB
Cartoons by O.V. Vijayan from *A Cartoonist Remembers*

ISBN: 978-81-291-0330-7

10 9 8 7 6 5 4 3

The moral right of the author has been asserted.

Printed at Rekha Printers Pvt. Ltd., New Delhi

Shahana Dasgupta, a graduate of Delhi University, holds an LLM degree from the University of Michigan, Ann Arbor, USA. She lives in Berlin, Germany, and has authored three *Rupa* publications for children—*This India*, *Razia: The People's Queen* and *Rani Lakshmibai: The Indian Heroine*.

"....may you grow up into a brave soldier in India's service."
Jawaharlal Nehru
in a letter to his daughter Indira on her thirteenth birthday.

"India simply cannot fail. We are all in this together.
It is not a question of this government or that government.
We simply cannot fail."
Indira Gandhi
7 November 1966

CONTENTS

PRIYA'S PROJECT

"MOST of us menfolk were in prison. Our women came to the front and took charge of the struggle....which not only took the British government but their own menfolk by surprise. It was not only that display of courage and daring, but what was even more surprising was the organizational power they showed."

Miss Chopra finished reading these lines from Jawaharlal Nehru's book, *The Discovery of India*. As she looked around the class a girl in the front row excitedly raised her hand. "I have heard my grandmother say the same thing. She remembers her mother often telling her about the huge public rallies she used to attend where women even from nearby villages could be seen shouting slogans against the British."

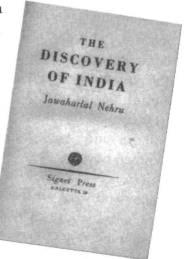

Miss Chopra nodded in agreement. "That's right," she said. "Women of that generation were passionately involved in the independence movement. It brought them out of their homes into public life. In fact when Gandhi made his famous call to Indian women to become politically active they responded enthusiastically."

"Well, girls, the next weeks we are going to work on a project," continued Miss Chopra. The entire class groaned inwardly at the thought of spending hours over dusty library books or piles of newspapers, reading about some obscure topic. But Miss Chopra's mind was already made up. She was a firm believer in project work which she thought, taught her students to gather information beyond that given in their textbooks. And Nehru's lines suddenly suggested to her the subject of her new project 'The Women of India'.

"The position of women in the family and in society has changed in the last 200 years. With the spread of education many new opportunities have opened up in different areas like medicine, law, business management, teaching, the media and of course, the ever popular computer sciences." Miss Chopra then went on to say how the poorer women had failed to march in step with those better off among the upper and middle classes. "Obviously there is much to be done, particularly in villages, and I want you to think about the many problems women have to face all over India. As daughters, wives, mothers and professionals—how do we see ourselves today and what are our dreams for tomorrow."

Miss Chopra paused. Her class of teenagers was beginning to get interested. Perhaps, a project on women did have an appeal after all.

A hand shot up, "Can we not talk just about Indian women in general but also the more famous among them?"

"Why not," said Miss Chopra encouragingly, "I want each one of you to write about the woman you admire most. Well, it could be someone well-known, a woman blessed with great talent, adored by millions; she might even be somebody not in the limelight but with distinct leadership qualities and a will to succeed against tremendous odds. You could choose from amongst queens and politicians, writers and poets, actresses and dancers, scientists and sportswomen. Let me see what you can come up with."

There were eager responses. "Rani of Jhansi," suggested somebody. "Lata Mangeshkar," said another girl. "Shabana Azmi", "Meena Kumari", "P.T.Usha", "Medha Patkar", "Aishwarya Rai", "Razia Sultan"....came a chorus of replies.

Miss Chopra smiled, "This promises to be very interesting," she said. "So let me make a note of your suggestions. Let me begin with you Priya. Who would you like to write about?"

Priya thought for a moment. She wanted to choose a modern personality—a woman of the times. Somebody who may have passed away but whose presence could still be felt, who lived on in people's memories and was the subject of their discussions and arguments.

Then she remembered the book that her grandfather had given her recently—'Glimpses of World History'. It was a series of about 200 letters written from prison by Jawaharlal Nehru to his young daughter Indira. Through them he presented the vast panorama of world history and the people who had shaped it. Priya had begun reading the book. Her interest in Indira Gandhi had been aroused by a conversation between her parents and grandparents about the war in the winter of 1971, from which Bangladesh emerged as an independent country on the eastern border of India. 1971 was a long time ago and yet Indira Gandhi seemed a living figure spanning the generations not only of her grandparents but also her parents.

"That is it," thought Priya. She had found the subject of her project. So when Miss Chopra, who had been waiting impatiently for her to reply, repeated, "Well Priya, have you decided?" Priya replied, "My choice is Indira Gandhi. She has been such a remarkable figure of modern India."

Miss Chopra noted down Priya's topic and then went on to the others. Her list of heroines grew longer and more varied, and began to sound like a Who's Who of Indian women down the years.

"Girls, get started quickly. I leave it to you to decide on the presentation. You could combine your text with photographs, recordings or drawings to make it more attractive. But please stick to the allotted length."

The school bell rang. Passing through the corridors Priya was still thinking of her project, and amidst the scraping of chairs and tables and the chatter of voices she neither noticed nor heard her best friend calling out to her. "Priya, shall we go down to the library today? I have chosen to write on Razia Sultan. I have no idea if there are any books on her, but I do remember seeing an old film about her on the television with Hema Malini in the title role."

"I wish there was a feature film on Indira Gandhi too," moaned Priya. "Instead I'll have to read through piles of books and newspaper articles and news magazines—all terribly dry stuff."

"You should be thankful," replied her friend, "sixteen years as prime minister means that you'll have a wealth of material to choose from. She doesn't really belong to the past, does she? She died hardly twenty years ago. I mean she's not history as yet. So if you only talked to your parents and grandparents you could begin your project straightaway. Your grandparents might even remember the young Indira Gandhi."

"Good idea," said Priya, "nevertheless the trip to the library is still on. Let's go."

That evening, her homework done, Priya sat down at the study table. In front of her was a small pile of books she had borrowed from the library. It had been difficult to choose from the large number of biographies, reminiscences, collections of letters and interviews, some only about Indira Gandhi's politics in the years she was in power. From these Priya had selected half a dozen books written by Ela Sen, Pupul Jayakar, K.A.Abbas, Inder Malhotra, M.J.Akbar and Mark Tully. She had also picked out two volumes, edited by Sonia Gandhi, of letters exchanged between Jawaharlal Nehru and his daughter.

Priya flipped through the pages of the first book, stopping every now and then to have a close look at the photographs. At one point she found herself staring at the well-known face of Indira with its alert yet distant and guarded expression, large eyes, sharp nose and a streak of grey hair.

The photographs showed her in different periods of her fascinating life with its tragic end. In such an event-packed story where was she to begin. The simplest way she finally decided, would be to start at the very beginning. So with the books ranged in front of her and pen and paper near at hand, Priya began her project.

PLAYING FREEDOM FIGHTER

IN 1917 Europe was in the midst of a world war, the First World War as it came to be known. Britain and its allies had already been in it for three long years, resulting in a heavy loss of men and material while fighting Germany and Austria. Exhausted and too preoccupied with the war, Britain was hardly able to devote any attention to ruling India. In India too, the war had been causing tremendous hardship. Not only were Indian soldiers fighting and dying for the British cause, but India was also being drained of vast amounts of money and raw materials to help the British war effort.

By 1917, rising prices and the lack of essential items began to affect the lives of ordinary Indians. Many found themselves slipping into poverty. There was also a mood of anger because while Indians were fighting abroad to defend Britain's interests, at home they were being denied any role in their own government. How could Britain, they asked, claim to be fighting a war in Europe to defend democracy and the rights of nations and yet not allow the same to India? The Congress party led the movement of protest but was still largely unconcerned with the increasing poverty amongst peasants and workers. The common man's growing resentment against the British was something the Congress party of those days failed to understand.

But a change came with the appearance of Mahatma Gandhi on the political scene. In 1915, in the midst of the war, he returned to India from South Africa. Sensing the angry mood of the millions he gave the Congress party a shape and direction which was later to turn into a mass movement for independence. In course of time Gandhi would challenge the Raj, by telling his countrymen that they only had to stop co-operating with the foreigners to make them leave India.

One-year-old Indira with her parents, Kamala and Jawaharlal Nehru.

The storm that was to sweep through India some years later under Gandhi's leadership was just gathering momentum in 1917, the year Indira Priyadarshini Nehru was born. Hers was an eagerly awaited birth. The large Nehru joint family had come together in Allahabad on a cold November day, certain that the first child of Jawaharlal Nehru and his young wife, Kamala, would be a son. The little baby turned out to be a girl, much to the disappointment of her grandmother, Swarup Rani. But her grandfather, Motilal, was delighted. "This daughter of Jawahar's, for all we know, may prove better than a thousand sons," he remarked.

Swarup Rani did not sulk for too long. Both she and Motilal were soon doting over their granddaughter. Motilal Nehru was a successful and highly respected lawyer who made a large fortune from his flourishing law practice. The family lived in style in a 37 roomed mansion called 'Anand Bhavan' in the exclusive European part of Allahabad, far away from the noise and smells of the old town where most Indians lived.

Priya stopped writing as she bent over the black and white photograph of Anand Bhavan which she had found in one of the library books. She saw a sprawling, elegant two-storeyed house with large windows, verandas and a small dome on the roof. It was surrounded by clumps of trees and what seemed to be very well-kept gardens. Priya could imagine the young Indira rushing in and out of the house, playing hide-and-seek in the garden and trying to climb the trees.

Priya was too engrossed in recreating the past when her grandfather came into the room. "Your mother wants you to lay the table. So, how's the school project getting along?" he asked.

"Grandfather, if Indira Gandhi had been alive today she would have been your age, wouldn't she?"

Grandfather nodded. "Perhaps slightly older."

"Why did Indira and her family get involved with the freedom struggle?" enquired Priya. "After all, Motilal Nehru was doing so well under the British Raj."

Priya's grandfather glanced at the photograph of Anand Bhavan lying on the table and answered, "When I was born the process of change had begun in our country. Gandhi had found the weapon with which to fight for independence. His idea of non-violence had captured the imagination of all Indians as the only way an unarmed and disarmed people could challenge British rule. Indians were not allowed to keep arms. Gandhi was anyway against violence of any kind. And this idea gradually gripped people throughout the country. It appealed to all of us—rich and poor, intellectuals and illiterates, villagers and town dwellers—as the only practicable way to fight, unarmed as Indians were."

Grandfather said that on one such unarmed gathering at Jallianwala Bagh in Amritsar the British fired indiscriminately killing hundreds. This incident in 1919 came to be known as the Jallianwala Bagh massacre. It stunned and outraged all. Many wanted to retaliate violently. Instead, Gandhi asked lawyers to give up their practice, merchants to stop selling foreign goods and parents not to send their children to British – run schools. There was to be non-violent non-cooperation as he called it.

The Mahatma changed India, and like most Indians the Nehrus too changed forever. So did the character of 'Anand Bhavan'. It became more Indian, less westernised and the display of wealth was toned down as well.

Anand Bhavan

The Jallianwala Bagh tragedy hit Motilal Nehru who had until then been largely uninvolved with the common man's problems. His young and restless son Jawaharlal, had already been attracted to Gandhi's message and unlike Motilal was uncompromising in his desire to get rid of the British. But after Jallianwala Bagh both father and son worked together towards Indian independence. And like others all over the country they too followed Gandhi's call to boycott the British courts and stop buying foreign goods.

"You seem to have collected quite a lot of books, Priya. Have you read about the incident where the Nehrus lit a huge bonfire of their foreign clothes?" grandfather asked.

"Yes," said Priya, "Years later Indira recalled the wonderful, colourful clothes going up in flames. It was a tough choice for a small girl of just three. A few days after the bonfire a relative presented Indira with a dress she had brought from Paris. As the family had taken to wearing khadi, Kamala Nehru wanted to return the gift. But she thought she would let her daughter decide, and Indira refused the dress. The relative was so cross at this refusal that she asked the little girl why she played with a foreign doll when she couldn't accept a foreign dress. The biting comment hit Indira hard. The doll was her pride and she was torn between her desire to keep it and the demands of her duty towards her parents. In the end she forced herself to throw her favourite doll into the flames. She too had done her bit for the freedom struggle."

The environment around Indira was one of excitement and enthusiasm but at the same time there was insecurity and uncertainty. The Nehru family's decision to join the freedom struggle meant that thereafter both Motilal and his son Jawaharlal, were every now and then fined, or arrested and thrown into prison. Anand Bhavan was frequently raided by the police who confiscated its furniture and carpets because of unpaid fines. It was the place where politicians and distinguished visitors came to debate and discuss the course of the freedom movement. All this Indira silently watched. She was probably too young to remember much—but some incidents certainly remained embedded in her memory.

"As a child," chuckled grandfather, "I remember spending many summer afternoons with other children creating stories about the freedom struggle. The older children were always eager to play the prized roles of freedom fighters. While the younger ones—

Sitting L-R Swarup Rani, Motilal, Kamala
Standing L-R Jawaharlal, Vijayalakshmi Pandit, Krishna, Indira,
Ranjit Pandit.

unfortunately—ended up with unwanted parts such as soldiers or policemen."

He continued, "Many years later when I read in a letter Nehru wrote from prison to his teenaged daughter that as a child she often pretended to be Joan of Arc, I was reminded of my own childhood. The story of the young Joan of Arc leading her people against the English must have greatly impressed little Indira. Like us, she too must have spent many a long afternoon re-enacting the political events that happened around her."

Indira's childhood was lonesome. Left to herself, she probably made her dolls provide her the company she missed in real life and recreate the world as she saw it, full of meetings, demonstrations and arrests.

Indira's unsettled childhood must have taught her to depend on her own strength. No wonder she developed into a fearless and independent character.

Little Indira standing in front of Lala Lajpat Rai.
Jawaharlal and Kamala Nehru are seen on her right.

Nehru encouraged his daughter to be fearless. In fact, both her parents did all they could to turn their shy little daughter into a bold girl. One of their methods was to ask her to go to her room after dinner all by herself. Indira had to hurry down a long dark veranda full of shadows and then up a flight of dimly lit stairs before she could reach her room to switch on the light. Understandably, she hated this daily test of nerves but she steeled herself to repeat it night after night.

Priya's conversation with her grandfather was interrupted by her grandmother. She had come to remind her husband that it was time for his daily medicines. "Come Dadi, sit here," said Priya. "Grandfather has been telling me about his childhood. Were you also in the habit of waving the flag as a young girl?"

"Oh those old days!" replied Priya's grandmother throwing her hands into the air. "Everybody wanted to be involved. I remember my mother and aunts organizing their day in such a way that after doing their share of house-work they would often go to public meetings, march in processions or picket shops."

"What did they do?" asked Priya curiously.

"My mother and a few other women would take turns to sit in groups in front of shops selling foreign cloth. They prevented customers from entering the shops and tried to persuade them not to buy the material. If a shopkeeper or customer refused to co-operate with them they would lie on the pavement in front of the shop or in front of the customer's car. This was called picketing. You must remember that until then it was not customary for women in our joint family to go about unescorted. And imagine, now they were lying on the road," said grandmother raising her eyebrows.

"All kinds of women volunteered to break the law in those days—rich and poor, educated and illiterate. The women of the Nehru family, for instance, especially Indira's mother Kamala, used to participate in these protests against the British Raj," she added.

When women in the Nehru household, including Kamala, joined the men in public demonstrations, Indira—then just seven years old—was left all to herself. She felt lonelier, more neglected than ever before and understandably grew more independent. When her grandfather and father began to spend long stretches of time in prison, Indira turned more and more to her mother. Mother and daughter became extremely attached to each other. But now with Kamala too in the thick of political struggle she desperately missed her presence. Yet, Indira was proud that her mother had finally chosen to be an activist. For Kamala it was an opportunity to

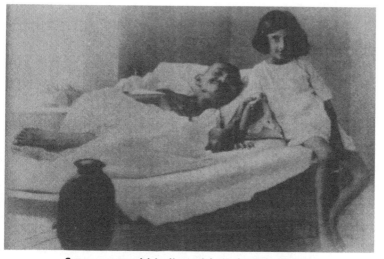

Seven-year-old Indira with Mahatma Gandhi.

make the Nehrus at last take notice of her and take her seriously.

"Indeed, the Kamala Nehru my mother saw and used to speak about," interrupted Priya's grandmother, "was an energetic and efficient organizer and a good speaker. Of course we knew nothing about the personal problems she had at that time. Only later on we learnt about Kamala's difficulties in adjusting herself to the ways of the westernised Nehru household. The unhelpful behaviour of some of the Nehru women had only increased her sense of neglect and isolation."

Young though she was, Indira sensed that her mother was being treated unfairly by them. So she stuck to Kamala through thick and thin all the more determinedly. It was due to her mother that despite the westernised atmosphere of the Nehru household, Indira became familiar with Indian values and customs, heard stories from the great Hindu epics and learnt to speak Hindi fluently. Kamala Nehru's short, unhappy life left its mark on Indira. Her mother's deep Indian roots influenced her forever.

"Enough of the past," said grandmother. "Will you lay the table, Priya? I think I heard your father coming in."

Priya nodded. As she put her books away her eyes fell on the photograph of a thin, awkward girl of about nine or ten years of age with a huge bow in her wavy hair. The girl stared solemnly into the camera. She did not look particularly happy or carefree but she appeared to be thinking and observing. "How truly the photographs reflect Indira," thought Priya, as she left the room.

THE SCHOOLGIRL

IT had been another one of those long tiring days when everything seemed to be going wrong. Already the morning had started badly for Priya. It began with a scolding from the geography teacher for having left behind her textbook at home. The day continued in the same unlucky fashion as she lost her favourite fountain pen, and ended just as miserably with a mathematics test which brought Priya to the point of despair.

She got off the school bus, heaved her heavy rucksack on her back and began the short walk home. The weather was quite bearable now. Over the weekend it had snowed a little too early in the hills of Mussoorie and the cold winds from there had lashed Delhi in the form of a hailstorm, sending the temperature tumbling to dampen the Dussehra fun.

The weeks between Dussehra and Diwali were Priya's favourite time of the year. With the heat of summer gone and the accompanying water shortage and power cuts over, she looked forward excitedly to festivals, good food, new clothes and lots of visitors.

"Would have been perfect," sighed Priya, "but today it has been such a terrible day." She groaned at the thought of piles of homework. Miss Chopra's project had to be done as well.

As she walked along slowly Priya wondered—did Indira Gandhi ever go to school? Did she have friends? Did she like mathematics? Was she good at sports? Was she expected to do well in school? Was school as important a factor in Indira's life as it was in hers ? Priya reached home, and rang the bell, still turning over the nagging questions in her mind.

"Ah, there you are," said her mother, opening the door. "I was wondering why you were taking so long. Wash your hands, lunch is ready." Priya gulped down her food hardly paying attention to what her mother was saying. Her mind was on Indira Gandhi for she was eager to find an answer to her questions.

In her room she rummaged through the material on her desk and finally found what she had been looking for. She picked up a letter written by a worried Jawaharlal to his father Motilal. "...Indira pays no heed to any kind of study....she must begin to acquire the habit of doing lessons. As it is she is past the age when she should have begun seriously."

Indira's education, Priya discovered, remained a problem. Finding a school for her was no easy task. Priya paused for a moment and then started writing what she had discovered.

Since the Congress had decided to boycott the British-run schools the Nehrus did not have much of a choice when it came to finding a suitable institution for Indira. For Motilal Nehru the Indian schools were not up to the standard and his son, Jawaharlal, feared that the British schools would turn his daughter into "a little Miss Muffet." In the end the little girl stayed at home and was taught by private tutors.

As a result she hardly had any contact with children of her own age. Mostly alone, she kept herself occupied by reading—dolls having given way to books. She was fond of fairy tales but her father who by now had started to get worried about his daughter's education, thought them a waste of time. Instead he wanted her to read books by authors such as H.G. Wells which unfortunately went way above her head. If she wanted to read fairy tales Indira had to do so in the bathroom or with a blanket over her head to avoid being discovered by her father. The trees in the garden of Anand Bhavan also provided excellent hiding places. Often Indira would take her books, climb up a tree and disappear behind the foliage while others frantically searched for her.

March 1926 brought changes in Indira's life. Her mother, never blessed with good health, fell ill with tuberculosis and doctors advised treatment in Switzerland. Indira was just over eight years of age when she and her parents left for Geneva. The noise and bustle of Anand Bhavan was left behind and for the first time she

Fourteen-year-old Indira.

had her parents to herself. The totally foreign environment which she now moved into also was a new experience for her.

Indira joined school and started travelling alone by tram and train in an unfamiliar city. Her mother naturally worried about the safety of her daughter. But the eight-year old showed that she was capable of looking after herself on the long journey to school. While Kamala Nehru tried to regain her health, Jawaharlal resumed his political activities—travelling to various parts of Europe to meet writers, scientists and statesmen. As a result the daily running of the household was shouldered by Indira. Soon she was handling the maid, paying school fees and shopping for groceries.

Jawaharlal encouraged his daughter to be out in the open as much as possible so that, as he wrote to her, "she would be like the deodars of the Himalayan forest, tall and straight and slender and graceful and at the same time strong." So from a simple activity like skipping, which he insisted she do regularly, Indira turned eagerly to more demanding sports like skiing, sledging and skating. No wonder she developed an interest in nature study. She also picked up French in school—a language she liked and often came back to in later years.

Although the time in Switzerland was in many ways one of the happiest in her life, and one which she was to remember very fondly, she did not find it easy to get closer to the other girls in school. Their hobbies and chatter seemed much too childish for her and she remained aloof.

Kamala Nehru gradually recovered and the family returned to India towards the end of 1927.

Back in Allahabad, Indira was sent to a convent school. The pretty dresses she had worn in Switzerland were now replaced by loose, rough khadi frocks. The other girls teased her about her unfashionable clothes, the teachers often scolded her and altogether Indira was unhappy.

On their part, Indira's father and grandfather were not impressed by the school. If she missed classes her grandfather would be unconcerned. He felt that the school did not teach anything worthwhile anyway. Every summer Indira used to go to the hills to escape the heat of the plains. This meant missing a part of the term and she would then have to struggle to make up. Motilal was not bothered, passing or failing in a subject seemed totally unimportant. But it did bother her father.

He noticed that Indira's mind was of a different kind. She would ask questions about everyday problems as well as about the more universal mysteries. "Why do toes bend downwards when we are walking?," she wrote to her father. " I have often noticed this while walking with chappals on, and try as I would to keep them straight they somehow bend."

Jawaharlal Nehru decided to take his daughter's education into his own hands. In 1928 in a series of letters—later published as *Letters of a Father to a Daughter*—he set about explaining to Indira the beginnings of the world and the origins of man. He taught her to appreciate the wonders of nature, pointing out to her the stars in the night sky and telling her how they came into existence. But he also took his daughter with him to important political meetings.

In 1928 Indira was present in Kolkata—Calcutta, as it was known then—at the annual session of the Congress party of which her grandfather had just been elected president. A year later she travelled to Lahore where the presidency passed from her grandfather to her father. Indira watched him astride a white horse as he rode into the Congress session. It was in Lahore in 1930 that full independence from Britain was declared as the aim of the national struggle. So for the twelve year old Indira, often absent from school, her father's hands-on approach to her education replaced the dull atmosphere of the classroom.

"Twelve years old," muttered Priya, "that's about my age. But our interests and worries could not have been more different." The book in front of her showed a photograph of Indira, thin and awkward, dressed in a white kurta and pyjama with a Gandhi cap worn at a slant on her head. This young girl was not concerned with studies or school. At twelve, her mind was elsewhere. She was now old enough to understand the momentous events that were happening around her and she wanted to participate in them.

Young Indira dressed in a white kurta and pyjama with a Gandhi cap with her parents, Jawaharlal and Kamala Nehru.

Indira applied for membership in the

Congress but was refused as she was too young. Angry at being shut out from the activities of the adults, she decided to set up a children's group which would assist the Congress workers. The 'Vanar Sena' as her band of boys and girls was called, distributed Congress bulletins, sewed flags, addressed envelopes, cooked meals, and occasionally carried secret messages to Congress workers in hiding or gathered information from the police. And of course, the children's brigade tried to keep fit with daily marching and drill.

From the diary kept by Indira at that time Priya jotted down with great interest the following extracts:

"September 6
Meeting of the Students' Working Committee
at 12.30.
Meet Gupta about Vanar Sena's work in
different wards.
Katra Vanar Sena's meeting at Katra Ashram from 6 pm
to 9 pm.
Drill and meeting of Vanar Sena and Bal Sangh at
Swaraj Bhavan at 5 pm."

Indira's capacity for organization impressed Priya. As she resumed her piece on Indira she noted a feature of Indira's character which in later years became more noticeable. She seemed to have a very clear idea of what to do.

In April 1930, Mahatma Gandhi started his Dandi march to the coast to collect salt as a symbolic defiance of the British law under which salt was a government monopoly. The defiance was supported by a wave of non-violent protest throughout the country. The British reacted with large-scale arrests and both Motilal Nehru

A group of women civil resisters. Indira and Kamala Nehru are
seated in the second row.

and his son were imprisoned.

From jail, Motilal wrote to his granddaughter, "What
is your position in the 'Vanar Sena'? I would suggest the
wearing of a tail by every member, the length of which
should be in proportion to the rank of the wearer. The
badge with the print of 'Hanuman' is all right , but see
that the 'gada', which is normally in Hanuman's right
hand is not there. Remember that the 'gada' means
violence and we are a non-violent army."

Sitting in jail, Jawaharlal Nehru's thoughts, however,
were on the more practical aspect of his daughter's future
career.

"I hope Indu is carrying on her studies regularly,"
he wrote to his wife. "She is and I am glad of it—a high-
spirited girl. I would rather have an ounce of spirit in her

than a pound of learning. But learning and mind training is also necessary and so I do hope that she will pay attention to these."

But for Indira, then actively involved with the 'Vanar Sena', going to school was farthest from her mind. She would not learn Sanskrit as it was a "dead language" and wrote to her father saying that she had decided to leave the much-disliked convent school. He insisted on Sanskrit but agreed to her leaving school. So once again teachers came home to instruct Indira.

The excitement of the times kept Indira busy and even happy. But it proved to be short-lived for in early February 1931, Motilal Nehru passed away. Without the indulgent and protective presence of her beloved grandfather Indira found life at Anand Bhavan quite unbearable.

Her parents then decided to send her to a small boarding school in Pune called 'The Pupil's Own School'. It was a period of uncertainty with most of the family including her mother in and out of jail.

Priya had written thus far when she spotted a letter from Jawaharlal Nehru to Indira shortly after her thirteenth birthday. In a low voice Priya read from the letter which Nehru must have written when his daughter was still in Allahabad packing her bags to leave for Pune. "You must be rather lonely. Once a fortnight you may see Mummy and once a fortnight you may see me...But I shall sit down with pen and paper and I shall think of you. And then you will silently come near me and we shall talk of many things."

The many letters written by Jawaharlal Nehru in the three years Indira spent in Pune must have meant a great deal to the young girl, far from home, weighed down by worries about her sick mother and a father who was in and out of prison. Apart from bringing world history and politics to his daughter, they showed her that she was constantly in her father's thought and although not physically present during much of her childhood, her father remained involved in her life and development.

The Pune school functioned as a school during the day but at night the rooms were converted into dormitories. The students were expected to help with daily jobs like cleaning, washing clothes and making beds. Indira found her day regulated by a school timetable which everyone was expected to follow.

Although she made a mark in school, becoming the president of the literary society and editor of the school magazine as well as 'chief justice' of the school committee, she remained, as in the past, a lonely figure.

Priya found another letter, this time written from Pune by Indira to her father in prison. Indira wrote:

"I imagine I'm skiing or having a snow fight and then, all of a sudden the snow and the happy rosy-cheeked Swiss children vanish and in their stead remain the hot rays of the sun, girls in five-yard saris, who cannot imagine what is the attraction of snow and who would far rather sit and talk than make snowmen.... It's nice to have some imagination. It's wonderful to fly anywhere you like in a second. But of course when somebody interrupts—I'm furious."

In April 1934, at the age of sixteen, Indira passed the school-leaving or matriculation examination. She was not very happy with her performance but she commented later, "I had inherited my grandfather's attitude: naturally I didn't want to fail, but it did not bother me too much."

Indira, after her arrival in Switzerland.

Meanwhile Nehru had planned his daughter's next step. He urged her to spend some time at Rabindranath Tagore's 'Visva- Bharati' in Santiniketan. Apart from learning languages, he thought, its excellent Fine Arts department would familiarize Indira with the cultural traditions of India.

Besides Santiniketan was a place to get to know people—students and teachers from all over the country, even from other parts of the world. Keeping this in mind, and fearing that his daughter would be branded a snob if she chose to stay separately with a cook and servant, Nehru insisted that she live with the others in the girl's hostel. "You must not put a barrier between yourself and the other students. Many of the girls there are very decent and you will soon be friends with them," he wrote.

Life in the hostel was as spartan as that in Pune. The students were expected to get up at dawn and take a cold

Indira at Santiniketan with Rabindranath Tagore.

bath even in winter. They had to clean their rooms and cook and serve community meals. Indira's fears that she would waste time washing clothes was countered by her father with the comment that, "a little washing was rather good for one."

Indira settled down to study English, Hindi, History, Civics and at her father's insistence—Chemistry. She also joined painting classes and started learning Manipuri dancing. Tagore's towering personality left a deep impression on her. Once she got over her initial shyness she joined other students as they sat under the trees and observed the great man at work. Later she was to describe these moments as "moments of supreme joy, memories to cherish."

Although an excited Indira, in a letter to her father described Santiniketan as, "artistic and beautiful and wild," her thoughts remained with her sick mother alone at home and her father who spent most of 1934 in the "other home". This was Nehru's term for prison. Indira made few friends and wrote to her father, "It is awful when surrounded by crowds and amidst all their chattering and playing, their rowdiness and noise, one has the feeling of being alone."

The year in Santiniketan came to an abrupt end in May 1935. Kamala Nehru needed urgent medical treatment in Germany and it was decided that Indira should accompany her mother abroad. After she left, Tagore wrote to Nehru, "It is with a heavy heart we bade farewell to Indira, for she was such an asset in our place. I have watched her very closely and felt admiration for the way you have brought her up."

Priya stopped writing and stared out of the window in front of her desk. She had been so preoccupied in the past hours that she had not even noticed how dark it was outside. The neighbourhood boys were returning home from the park swinging their cricket bats. A couple of girls went by chatting loudly and breaking into an

occasional giggle. Returning birds settled down for the night in the small jacaranda tree across the road. But Priya's thoughts were still on Nehru and his daughter.

She pictured Jawaharlal Nehru sitting in Almora jail staring out into the darkness. He had seen so little of his daughter in the past years and as she set sail for Europe in those uncertain times he must have wondered when and where he would see her again. Priya recollected lines from an earlier letter from father to daughter:

> "Priyadarshini, dear to the sight," wrote Nehru, "but dearer still when sight is denied."

THE YOUNG WOMAN

PRIYA hurried to the nearby grocery store dodging bicycles and cars as she crossed the road. It was her turn every evening to help with the household chores, and normally she combined it with a game of badminton or a walk in the park with one of the neighbourhood girls. But dusk had fallen and there was a nip in the air. So she quickly collected the packets of milk, paid for the 'jalebis' and headed home. Sitting at her desk a little later with a mug of milky, steaming tea and a few 'jalebis', she picked up where she had stopped some time ago—tracing Indira's years in Europe.

It was a reserved but capable and determined young woman who set sail from Mumbai—Bombay as it was then named—in May 1935. Indira had not yet turned eighteen, she however assured her father that she would be able to look after her sick mother. "You have no business to do otherwise, for you have the family reputation to keep up," was her father's immediate reply.

As the European summer set in, Kamala Nehru seemed to respond positively to the medical treatment.

Her daughter settled down too. Although she noticed the atmosphere of uncertainty in Germany as if it was on the verge of war with aeroplanes flying overhead all the time and searchlights at night. She began to think about her future, about going to a university and the subjects she would want to study.

Encouraged by her father—who continued to guide her through his letters from prison—Indira decided to learn German and brush up her French at the Swiss school she had attended many years ago as a child. Both father and daughter thought that it would be a good place to prepare for university entrance examinations.

Adjusting to life in Europe also meant throwing overboard the 'Santiniketan look'. "It is awful going out in a sari," she wrote to her father. "Everybody turns round and stares and looks me up and down, till I want to just sink in the ground....I have ordered two dresses." And then she continued, "Yesterday afternoon I went and had my hair cut, partly because it was hot and partly because my 'jura' became untied about ten times a day and it was a nuisance making it."

Although Indira tried to settle down at her old school she found it hard to do so. She was older than the other girls. Fitting into the regimented schedule

Young Indira with her parents, Jawaharlal and Kamala Nehru.

of a school had always been a problem for her. Now that she was older, she was fed up with living by rules and wanted to be free to organize her day as she chose to.

But the responsibility of looking after her mother also tied her down. Kamala Nehru's health which seemed to have been improving took a turn for the worse and Indira sensed that time was running out for her mother. Desperate and alone she telegraphed her father who was then released from prison in September 1935 and allowed to visit his critically ill wife. Nehru arrived in Europe. But even then he spent only part of his time with his family. The rest was spent travelling to London and Paris trying to win support for India's demand for independence.

Kamala Nehru was moved from Germany to Switzerland where she died on 28 February 1936.

In the last months of her life she got sympathy and companionship from a young Parsi student named Feroze Gandhi. He was studying at the London School of Economics and would visit her whenever he had the time. Feroze, a staunch supporter of the freedom movement, was known to her from the early days in Allahabad when she was passionately involved in Congress activities. He had come to admire and appreciate Kamala Nehru

as a brave and likeable person whom he tried to help in whatever way he could. Over the years Feroze Gandhi had also become a familiar and faithful figure in the lonely and chaotic world of Kamala's daughter.

Meanwhile he had fallen in love with Indira and spoken to Kamala of his feelings for her daughter. Kamala was fond of the open, lively and reliable young man and had no doubt that if married to Feroze, her daughter would be in safe hands. But Indira, although aware of Feroze's interest in her and the trust her mother placed in him, was not prepared to commit herself.

In her short life burdened by poor health and complicated by personal problems Kamala Nehru realised that she had not always been able to give her daughter the care and guidance that the girl needed. Nevertheless, she had tried her best, and her death at the age of thirty-six left in Indira a wound which never healed. Years later

Indira at Zurich, 1937

Indira commented that "the scar and the effect of it are always there in some way....I do think of her as if she were here quite often."

"If only I could find a photograph of Indira of those days," thought Priya as she quickly turned over the pages of one of the biographies in front of her. Instead of a photograph she came across lines written by a friend of Nehru's which portrayed Indira far more effectively than any photograph could have, "a thin, desperate adolescent... a pathetic figure—though young in years—old beyond her years in experience and suffering."

Nehru left his daughter alone in Europe and returned to India soon after his wife's death, causing Mahatma Gandhi to write to the eighteen-year old Indira, "Kamala's passing away has added to your responsibilities but I have no misgivings about you. You have grown sufficiently wise to understand your dharma completely. Kamala possessed qualities rarely found in other women....May God give you long life and strength to emulate her virtues."

Back in India, Jawaharlal Nehru took over as president of the Congress party at a difficult moment. In 1937 the British parliament had decided to hold elections to the provincial legislative assemblies in order to begin at last the process of self-government which had been promised to India so repeatedly. The Congress had been split on the issue of whether to participate in the elections, Nehru being against it. In the end Nehru gave way, putting the unity of the Congress above all.

So, he plunged into campaigning, tirelessly travelling the length and breadth of the country, getting to know it and its people. Personal hardships seemed to fade and become unimportant for him when placed beside the struggle to free India, or the suffering of the millions of his countrymen.

Priya had wondered how Nehru could leave his daughter alone and return to India soon after the tragic loss of her mother. But she now understood that he had a greater purpose in mind, a more exciting dream which he wanted his daughter to share. In December 1938, Nehru wrote to his daughter who was still in Europe,

"Many years ago I used to dream that when you grew up, you would play a brave part in what is called public life in India, to shoulder this heavy burden, to help in putting brick upon brick in the building of the India of our dreams. And I wanted you to train and fit yourself in body and mind for this engrossing task."

Nehru had been nudging Indira to think about her future in terms of serving India. He believed that a European university education would widen her horizon and prepare her for a life in public service. Accordingly he arranged for her to go to Badminton School in Bristol, England so that she could prepare for admission to Oxford University.

Before leaving for Bristol, Indira spent a few months in London sharing a flat with an old school friend from

Pune. She loved the city and enthusiastically set about exploring its sights and its rich cultural life. She visited museums, went to concerts, plays and films, and enjoyed dining with her father's important friends and acquaintances. Indira also got involved in politics, joining Krishna Menon's India League.

But above all, she enjoyed the freedom of being an independent young woman in a big, lively city. She wrote to her father, "A tiny little room to sleep in—the whole city to live in and no one to bother about you—to go and come and do whatever you want to. Sometimes it was lonely but I liked it. If only one would not miss some people so much."

The months in London came to an end and October 1936 found a reluctant Indira in Badminton School. The British novelist Iris Murdoch who was a student there at that time recalled Indira as somebody "who was extraordinarily beautiful, but looked very frail. She was a very dignified and aloof girl, but it was obvious to all of us that she was very unhappy and couldn't wait to get back to her country. She didn't like the school very much...."

Iris Murdoch's observations were not inaccurate. For while in Bristol, Indira was complaining to her father that she was lonely and did not have any real friends. Nobody seemed to understand her and accept her as she was. She found it difficult to get along with the English schoolgirls. "Everybody seems to talk for the sake of talking. I hate chatting—unless I have something to say," she wrote.

Fortunately, Indira's loneliness at school was made bearable by the presence, in England, of Feroze Gandhi. His was a familiar face and the warm relationship he had had with Kamala Nehru formed a bond between him and Indira. Although they came from totally different backgrounds and had almost opposing personalities, they got along well with one another. Indira now saw him in a different light and began to think about marriage and settling down with Feroze.

"I feel I have changed tremendously since you last saw me—I cannot describe it to you and I do not know if you will notice it for it is not expressed outwardly," she wrote to her father from England.

While Indira attended courses in history and anthropology at Oxford from 1937, she took great interest in world politics and was very left-wing in her ideas and opinions. She joined the Indian Majlis—a society of Indian students and the University Labour Club. Indira was an active if silent member of political organizations but being the daughter of a famous and eloquent father she often found herself in uncomfortable situations. On one such occasion, she was asked by Krishna Menon of the India League to read out a message from her father and say a few words at a public meeting. Indira's inborn shyness left her tongue-tied. She found herself unable to utter a

Indira with her father

word—much to the amusement of a man in the audience who remarked, "She does not speak, she squeaks."

Priya could not help laughing as she read about the embarrassing incident. As she continued reading and taking notes, she was surprised at the modern tone of the letters written from England by Indira to her father.

They were so typical of a student of today that Priya could easily relate to Indira. For her, Indira Gandhi ceased to be a remote figure and became a normal, familiar young person subject to examination fever, and nervousness, but at the same time itching for fun and dreaming of romance.

"Yesterday I had a terribly full day," wrote Indira to her father. "I had to go out in the morning—then at two there was a Labour study group." She was referring to a meeting of the British Labour Party members. "At three fifteen Basil Mathews and his wife came and took me to their house on Boar's Hill for tea. I got back at six forty-five—at seven I was having supper with 'The Darb' (Miss Darbyshire).... I got home at eleven fifteen p.m.—just in time not to be locked out! My essay on the Evolution of Parliament had to be read at a class at ten a.m. this morning and until eleven fifteen last evening I had not even read about it! Well, I read until twelve forty-five and then wrote until three fifteen a.m. It was a job getting up this morning—I missed signing the register as well as my breakfast, for I was ready only just in time for a lecture at ten a.m.! However I got Very Good for the essay!"

Examinations over, Indira left for a well-earned rest and a skiing holiday. "I packed up a rucksack, slung it on to my back, got into my ski trousers and big boots and here I am.... When I first arrived the snow was not too good but then it snowed all day and night and Gosh what snow! I have never enjoyed skiing so much. I left London with the intention of trying skating as well as skiing—but skiing leaves no time for anything else."

Towards the end of 1939, Indira fell ill with a lung infection and fears that she would be plagued by chest disease as her mother had been, prompted her to leave Oxford and seek treatment in Switzerland. She did not return to college again and was to remain in Switzerland for nearly a year.

For her, personally it was a happy, busy time though interrupted by her own poor health and overshadowed by the rapidly approaching war in Europe. At home in India, the freedom struggle was coming to a head and Indira's thoughts were often with her father sitting in silent, empty Anand Bhavan. She longed to participate in the struggle and be at her father's side.

In the end all these factors were to combine to cut short her stay in Oxford and she was to return to India without an academic degree but as a wholly changed person.

In September 1939 the war had engulfed Europe. While the British fought they were in no mood to be distracted by problems in India. Instead they wanted India—as in the past—to support their war efforts. This was a point which Nehru was no longer prepared to accept. His demand was that if the British wanted India as an ally then they must give her the status of an ally which meant that they would have to transfer power to the Indians immediately. On 30 October 1940, Jawaharlal Nehru gave a stirring speech in Gorakhpur. He was arrested thereafter, charged with 'anti-government propaganda' and sentenced to four years imprisonment.

The turmoil of war and her father's arrest convinced Indira that the time had come to return home. She felt that at twenty-two she was ready to plunge into the freedom movement and into marriage. Accompanied by Feroze, she set sail from a war-torn London in early 1941 and reached Mumbai a few months later in April. The years in Europe had come to an end.

Indira returned to a much-changed Anand Bhavan. In the years that she had been abroad her grandmother and grand-aunt had passed away, and with them the last of the old generation. Anand Bhavan itself was locked up and uninhabited as her father was in Dehradun jail.

On her arrival Indira lost no time in telling her father of her decision to marry Feroze Gandhi. Nehru was shocked. At meetings in prison and through letters he tried to convince his daughter to reconsider the step, pointing to the enormous differences in background and mentality between her and Feroze.

Feroze Gandhi

Besides Nehru had plans and dreams for his daughter, wanting her to follow the family tradition of public service. He hoped to, as he wrote to Indira, "gently, slowly but surely to train your mind in that wider understanding of life and events that is essential for any big work." An early and hasty marriage, he feared, would put a halt to these plans and tie her down to the routine of domestic life.

But Indira stuck to her decision, defending it against her father's objections, as well as facing a storm of protest from conservative Hindus all over the country. The news that Nehru's daughter was about to enter into an inter-faith and inter-community marriage with a Parsi caused a furore in India, forcing both Nehru and Mahatma Gandhi as a protective gesture to publicly support the union.

In the end, the wedding took place in March 1942 in Allahabad. The bride wore pink. It was a cotton sari hand woven from the yarn spun by her father in jail. Anand Bhavan had been spruced up for the occasion and Nehru,

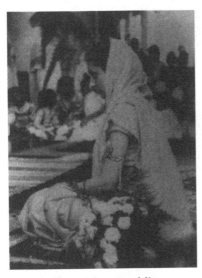

Indira at her wedding.

released from prison a few months earlier, played host to guests who included relatives and friends, nationalist leaders and some foreigners. One of them was Sir Stafford Cripps, representative of the British government who was in India at that time. At dinner the preoccupied bride but thoughtful hostess asked him to take a second helping. "Do have some potato cripps, Sir Stafford," Indira stuttered.

After a brief honeymoon in Kashmir the young couple settled down in Allahabad. Nehru's fears proved baseless, for although Indira attended to household chores she did not give up political activities. Meanwhile as the war raged in Europe, in India too it was a time of crisis. On 7 August 1942 the Congress passed the Quit India resolution. The next day Gandhi, Nehru and other

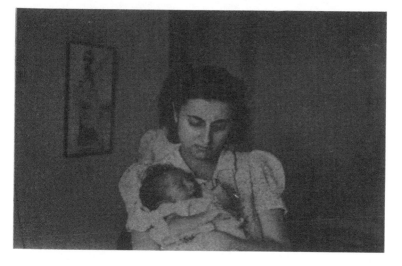

Congress leaders were put in prison. The absence of their leaders did not stop thousands from carrying on the struggle spontaneously in the form of public demonstrations, strikes and, in certain areas of the country, even violent action which brought the administration to a standstill. The British came down heavily on the people in an attempt to stifle the movement by arresting thousands and mercilessly breaking up demonstrations and meetings.

In September 1942 Indira herself was arrested while making a speech at a meeting in Allahabad. Feroze and many others who were present followed her into prison. For Indira this was a moment which she was to describe later as the "most dramatic incident" in her life. "I had made up my mind that I had to go to prison. Without that...something would have been incomplete."

She spent nine months behind bars sharing the ward with her aunt Vijaylakshmi Pandit and her cousin Chandralekha. Life was harsh, uncomfortable and dull.

As the seasons passed and one day merged into another the women tried to break the monotony of jail life by reading, acting out plays or learning languages. Indira amused herself by giving funny names to the animals that crept through the cell at night. There was Bartholomew the Bat and Minto and Morley Musk-rat and the cats— Mehitabel and Marmaduke—and their kittens— Kanhaiya, Moti and Parvati. This dreary existence came to an end in May 1943 when Indira was released from prison because of ill-health.

She left the Naini jail to return to Anand Bhavan. Her father was still in prison but Feroze her husband was released a few months later. Indira and Feroze settled down in Anand Bhavan where Indira kept herself busy doing up the place and giving the old house a fresh look. But her mind was with her father to whom she wrote long letters and who was delighted that his daughter was

Indira with her aunt Vijaylakshmi Pandit, Eleanor Roosevelt and Pandit Nehru

shaping up just the way he had always wanted her to.

"From the closed house that was herself, she is looking out more and finding a new interest and new excitement in the world," he wrote in his diary.

Nehru was still in prison when Indira gave birth to her first son, Rajiv, in August 1944. It was a joyful moment in Indira's life for she believed that for a woman motherhood was the highest fulfilment.

In summer 1945 Nehru was released from prison. The war in Europe was over. The British government started talks with the Congress, and Nehru's presence was needed. Indira left her year-old son and accompanied her father.

As the negotiations over partition and independence continued Nehru was determined to have his daughter beside him in Delhi. Father and daughter were now a team - partners though in different roles in shaping the future of the country. In the midst of all this political activity, Indira's second son Sanjay was born in December 1946.

Priya leant back in her chair and browsed through the pages she had written so far. Her story of Indira Gandhi had reached a turning point and she needed a

Indira with Jawaharlal Nehru and Rajiv

photograph that showed the new woman who had emerged out of childhood and adolescence. She studied the pictures of Indira on her wedding day, with her husband, and with her father and sons. They portrayed a new Indira, no longer shy and awkward but elegant and self-confident although still rather reserved and somewhat stern. Here was a young woman approaching the final year of her twenties—wife, mother and closest adviser to her father who was to become the first prime minister of India. Priya could not help thinking that it was the face of somebody who meant business and was waiting to prove herself.

HER FATHER'S DAUGHTER

DIWALI had come and gone and it had turned rather cold. The mornings were grey and foggy and when Priya waited for the school bus she could scarcely see the houses in front of her. Often it was almost noon before the pale sun's rays managed to struggle through the cold damp air that hung over Delhi. At school the old classrooms with their high ceilings and stone floors were equally unwelcoming. On such days Priya was glad to get home and sink into the cosy warmth of a pile of blankets.

But today the sky was blue and despite the wind Priya felt like basking in the warm sun. It was a Friday afternoon and the weekend stretched ahead of her, so there was no need to hurry. On her way back from school she stopped to buy some roasted peanuts. As she cupped her hands around the warm packet of nuts, she could think of nothing nicer than spending the afternoon reading a novel, munching peanuts and lazing around.

She reached home to find her mother waiting at the gate. "Priya," she said in a suspiciously chirpy fashion, "there you are. The other day you mentioned Teen Murti Bhavan in connection with your project. I thought it would be a good idea to go and see it—should be interesting as well. Today is just the right day for such an outing—pleasant weather and the fresh air should do you good. Take an exercise book and a pen along and I'll lend you my camera. If we leave soon, we should be back before dusk."

Priya saw her 'lazy afternoon' being replaced by her mother's idea of 'interesting'. "This sounds more like Miss Chopra's educational trips", she muttered as she grabbed a sandwich, put a few things into her rucksack and reluctantly got into the car.

Teen Murti Bhavan used to be the residence of the British Commander-in-Chief, before India's first prime minister moved into it in 1947 just after independence. Indira and her husband, Feroze Gandhi, had left Allahabad for Lucknow where Feroze was working with a newspaper and for a while Indira commuted between Lucknow and Delhi. But the thought of her father having to fend for himself in Delhi proved unbearable. The prime minister's job was a very demanding one and she wanted to take some of the burden off her father. So whenever he sent a telegram asking her to help out as hostess, she rushed to Delhi. Besides, helping her father meant that she remained at the centre of Indian politics. For a woman who had grown up with politics, being cooped up as just wife and mother in faraway Lucknow was out of the question.

So shortly after Nehru moved to Teen Murti Bhavan he was joined by his daughter and grandsons. Indira ran the household and was both hostess and travelling companion to her father. It was the beginning of a momentous period of seventeen years in which she was to witness the death of some of those closest to her. But it was also a time which she fully utilised to carve out for herself a position in national politics. When the opportunity came it enabled her to stake her own claim to the top job.

Now it was Feroze who had to do the commuting. He visited his sons regularly, until in 1952 he was elected a member of parliament and moved from Lucknow into his own bungalow in the capital, for he was unwilling to be seen as taking advantage of being the prime minister's son-in-law. But despite his being in Delhi, Indira and the children continued to live in Teen Murti Bhavan.

It did not take Priya and her mother too long to reach the tree-lined Teen Murti Marg. Having parked the car they passed through the tall gates and into the sprawling grounds of Teen Murti Bhavan. Avoiding the huge shady trees that lined the wide curved driveway, they chose to stroll in the sunshine along the edge of the well-kept lawns. It was such a peaceful scene. Gardeners were busy

Teen Murti Bhavan

trimming the bougainvillea shrubs, birds pecked in the grass, disturbed only by the occasional squirrel that scampered by, and a group of women chatted on the steps leading up to the broad veranda that formed the entrance to the palatial residence.

"What a graceful house!" exclaimed Priya's mother admiringly, as she looked up at the impressive golden sandstone front. As they walked through the drawing-room on the ground floor, Priya was puzzled by her mother's enthusiastic comments. She looked at the enormous room, with its towering walls and ceiling, kept as it had been in Nehru's time, and wondered whether the guests would have had to yell out to each other in order to make themselves heard. Priya found the endless corridors rather unnerving as well. On the whole, she thought the place was too big and overpowering—there was nothing homely about it. So she asked her mother why she liked it so much.

"Over fifty years ago this mansion was home to two small children and they must have enjoyed these wide open grounds and the spacious rooms. I am sure they never felt fenced in, and for little boys what could be nicer than that!"

"Besides", continued her mother as they looked across the gardens, "Nehru, his daughter and grandsons shared a love for animals and had a sort of mini zoo over here. Apart from dogs, parrots and squirrels they kept a number of exotic pets. Amongst them was the family favourite—a red Himalayan panda called 'Bhimsa' who used to live in the boys' bathroom, before a cage was built for him in the garden. Then there were three tiger cubs—Bhim, Bhairav and Hirimba.

"There is another interesting story connected with the garden. As a small boy Rajiv's occasional outbursts used to irritate his mother. She explained to him that his behaviour disturbed her, and that if he wanted to cry or yell he should go to the fountain in the garden and do so. Thereafter whenever the need arose, Indira would whisper 'fountain' and Rajiv would disappear into the garden to let out his anger. I am sure this house and its grounds were a paradise for children."

Back inside the house mother and daughter went through the exhibition of photographs, cuttings and letters which documented Nehru's life and Priya found that many photographs were familiar to her for she had come across them in the library books.

The two then passed by the modest bedrooms of Indira and her father. Indira's room had the essential pieces of furniture but there was nothing fussy or opulent about it. Priya thought it fitted Indira's personality—frugal, controlled, rational and giving little of herself away. She did notice a photograph of Rabindranath Tagore on the wall, though.

Priya heard her mother calling out to her to come and see some of the gifts given to Nehru by visiting dignitaries. As they looked at the items on display she tried to imagine the many powerful, famous and glamorous people who had walked through the rooms. Amongst them were Chou-en Lai and Nikita Khrushchev—the prime ministers of China and the Soviet Union, Eleanor Roosevelt and Jacqueline Kennedy—wives of American presidents and Lady Mountbatten, the wife of the last Viceroy.

Indira ran a busy household. She was responsible for settling guest lists and menus for meals, staff salaries and taking care of the animals on the compound. It is said that the task she disliked most was putting menus together. She complained of the peculiar eating habits of Indians—of meat-eaters who were vegetarians on certain days of the week, of some vegetarians who ate eggs and still others who ate fish.

Indira among her guests.

In London with father Jawaharlal Nehru.

Her father's enthusiasm for picking up new customs and recipes abroad and introducing them at home added to her problems. After dining at Buckingham Palace Nehru took to the Palace's way of serving milk and sugar before the coffee. But when it was introduced in Teen Murti Bhavan, Indira found embarrassed guests hurriedly looking around to see whether they had forgotten or misplaced their coffee.

All these little incidents and details related by her mother amused Priya. "Life with her father must have been rather stressful at times. I wouldn't have expected a prime minister to bother about such household matters," she said.

Priya and her mother had finished their tour and now stood at the back of the house in front of a small clump of trees. It was twilight and the evening mist had brought the winter's day to an early end. Amidst the foliage on the ground they could see the eternal flame burning in memory of Nehru.

Priya walked back to the car. It had not been a bad idea to come after all. The visit had helped her fit one more piece into the puzzle.

On reaching home Priya spread her little collection of Nehru family photographs to see if there was any of Indira with her father and sons in the Teen Murti gardens. She was finally able to spot one in one of the books. There they were—deep in conversation—Indira with flowers in her hair, Nehru with a rose in his buttonhole and between them a rather sulky Rajiv. Now that Priya had been to Teen Murti Bhavan, the photographs seemed to come alive. She resumed reading and taking notes.

Independence day in August 1947 was one of the proudest and most satisfying moments in Indira's life. This was reflected in an interview some years later when she said, "Young people don't remember this, but the worst part of being under foreign rule was the constant humiliation. Going to jail or being beaten up was a very small part of our suffering. The really galling part was that you were constantly being humiliated in your own country."

She was present in the parliament when at midnight of 14 August 1947 her father made his famous "tryst with destiny" speech. The next day—with the same feeling of disbelief that the impossible had finally happened—she saw him raise at the Red Fort the national flag modelled on the Congress party flag he had raised seventeen years ago at Lahore.

The price that India paid for freedom was partition and the violent communal riots that followed. In 1947 Delhi was full of thousands of Hindu and Sikh refugees and Indira started working amongst them in the refugee camps. One day she saved the life of an old Muslim man who was being chased by a mob. On hearing about the incident, Gandhi suggested that she go to the Muslim areas of Delhi and report to him on the situation there. Indira was shocked to see the plight of the Muslims, and as the Mahatma had asked her to, she worked hard to improve the living conditions in these areas.

Indira saw the Mahatma for the last time a day before he was assassinated. He was wearing an old hat and was in a relaxed mood. They talked about films while Rajiv played with the great man's toes, trying to wind a string of jasmine flowers around them. The next day the dearly loved face was gone. Someone she had known from childhood, and with whom she had disagreed on many occasions, but also turned to frequently for advice and comfort was no longer there. She was to say later, "He was so much a part of our family and of India that we simply couldn't imagine India without him…. It was such a comfort to know that he was somewhere in the country and that you could reach out to him."

Gandhi's death left Nehru without a guiding hand that could show him the way through the maze of problems that faced the nation. While tackling a host of issues on the domestic front , Nehru also set about establishing for India the place and importance it deserved in world politics. By then the nations of the world had become divided between two opposing groups, one led by the United States and the other by the Soviet Union as Russia was then known. Nehru's policy was to keep India away from both these groups. This was the policy which later came to be known as non-alignment and which won him respect and recognition abroad, especially in Asia and Africa. As a statesman of stature he attracted many world leaders to Teen Murti Bhavan and Nehru himself travelled widely.

Indira accompanied him on most of his visits which took her to the United States, China, Indonesia and the Soviet Union. On one of the many trips to Britain she found herself sitting next to the formidable Winston Churchill. The ageing British prime minister remarked, "Isn't it strange that we should be talking as friends, when we hated each other such a short while ago?" "But Sir Winston, we never hated you personally," replied Indira. Embarrassed, Sir Winston could only say "But I did, I did!"

In her role as hostess Indira not only got to know personally the leading players in world politics, but became familiar with the complicated issues of world politics. It was an invaluable education. With time she was able to press on her father her own views on foreign affairs and sometimes even take matters into her own hands.

One such occasion was during the war with China in 1962. The Chinese army had advanced deep into Indian territory in the northeast and threatened the plains of Assam. A disheartened Nehru had not expected the Chinese to act so violently. And he could see no way out. The military and administration in the state felt equally powerless. The civilian population found themselves abandoned by the authorities.

The thought of leaving defenceless people to their fate and of buckling under foreign pressure was unacceptable to Indira. Totally fearless, she travelled under difficult circumstances to Tezpur in Assam, to reassure the civilians and organize help for them. Nehru worried about the safety of his daughter. But he felt helpless. When others pointed out that she was being very obstinate he pleaded, "You know Indira. Once she has decided who can stop her." This tough side of her character she displayed on many occasions in later years, showing tremendous leadership and determination at times of crisis.

It was in her capacity as the prime minister's daughter that Indira revealed her talent for politics, as well as the ambition, nerves and energy to take it up as a career. She felt it within her that the best way to serve her country was through politics.

Indira was by now fed up of the social work she had been doing, complaining to her father, "I do want to reorganize my life and get out of all the silly committees. I am so sick of people doing social work as a step up the political and social-set ladder, and equally sick of the vague goodness of the so-called Gandhians." In the 1952 general elections she campaigned for her father—advising him, travelling to remote places to address rallies and helping with the organization of the campaign.

She was to recount one such incident during the campaign. "It was a cold and misty January morning with a sharp breeze and at six a.m. still quite dark. Not a soul was in sight. All doors and windows seemed to be tightly secured. However there was a 'takht', a microphone and some 'dhurries', wet with dew. Hansrajji felt that we had done our duty by coming and could now drive on....I insisted on giving a speech whether there was anybody to listen or not. Almost with my first word, windows started banging open and tousled heads appeared. Immediately afterwards the entire village poured out from the warmth of their houses, wrapped in blankets and 'razais', some with 'datun' sticks and some with tumblers of steaming tea."

As the prime minister's daughter Indira was keen to protect her father from unwanted visitors. She was also concerned about his health and, whenever possible, she tried to lessen his heavy workload. Nehru's tight schedule did not allow him to meet everybody and often it was left to his daughter to listen to Congress leaders and other politicians, and sort out their problems. As she became more involved she learnt to steer her way through the intricacies of Congress party politics, rapidly rising to the top of the party.

In 1959, at the age of forty-two Indira was elected President of the Congress party. She was to say that it was a most important event in her political life. Although Nehru did not think it was a good thing for his daughter to become Congress president while he was still prime minister, he was very proud of her elevation to the post. While attending a party meeting under her presidency he said, "At first Indira was my friend and adviser, then she became my companion and now she is my chief."

One of Indira's most controversial actions as party president was to intervene in the state politics of Kerala, thereby setting a dangerous precedent of putting party interests before anything else. The Communists had won the state elections, thus breaking the Congress party's moncpoly of power in regional politics. Indira was unhappy about it, fearing that once out of power the Congress would cease to play any role in Kerala. She decided to topple the state government and in the process abandoned the Congress party's secular ideals by joining right-wing and communal parties in order to stir up the anti-communist agitation in the state.

By now Indira had the confidence and ear of the prime minister. So much so that Nehru, although unhappy about his daughter's tactics, reluctantly agreed with her to ask the President of India to suspend the legally elected Communist government, and bring Kerala under President's rule. Fresh elections were held. Indira took a totally pragmatic attitude. Elections had to be won at all costs. The same Congress party which in the past had vowed never to form an alliance with a communal party like the Muslim League, went back on its word. Together the two parties managed to defeat the Communists.

Once again Indira had shown her decisive and tough nature. Although her politics won Congress the Kerala elections, she came in for much criticism, for having thrown overboard all principles. One of her strongest critics was her husband, Feroze Gandhi.

Feroze was by now a respected and capable member of parliament, having won the Rae Bareilly constituency in the 1952 general elections. But his personal life was far from happy. After his marriage to Indira in 1942 he had spent a few harmonious years in Lucknow with his wife and sons. He doted on the boys and they in turn were very attached to him. Both parents tried to spend as much time as possible with the children and despite occasional quarrels due to their contrasting personalities, they continued to live as a normal, young family.

But Feroze knew that it was only a matter of time before the yearning for her father and the lure of politics would pull Indira away from him. The relationship between Indira and her father had always been a very strong one. As her father grew older, and especially after her mother's death, Indira wanted to be near him and to take care of him. And then there was the fascinating world of politics without which she felt she was not in her element. So in 1947, when Indira took the children and left for Delhi, from Feroze's point of view the inevitable split had happened.

Although he moved to Delhi a few years later and saw his sons regularly, Indira and Feroze had drifted apart. So much so that even on some political issues they were at loggerheads. Feroze was furious about his wife's role in the Kerala crisis. A devoted parliamentarian, he lobbied persistently against this style of power politics— much to Indira's anger.

Towards the end of his life, Feroze suffered from poor health. His first heart attack worried Indira, and the thought of losing him briefly brought them together. But it was a little too late. Feroze died in September 1960, a few days short of his forty-eighth birthday. Her husband's

Indira with her husband, Feroze Gandhi.

Father and
daughter
walking on the
lawns of Teen
Murti Bhavan.

untimely death came as a great shock to Indira and for awhile she was totally devastated. She was aware that despite their differences Feroze had been by her side at times of difficulty and need. Although in later years Indira never spoke about her husband publicly she once told friends, "The Nehrus were very unmusical people. It was Feroze who introduced us to the joys of western classical music."

In order to get over his death, Indira returned to politics as soon as possible. She was now a widow with two teen-aged sons and an increasingly weary father. The Chinese invasion of India in 1962 hastened the decline in Nehru's health. He had invested much in the policy of co-operation with China and genuinely believed that he had succeeded in establishing friendly relations between the two great countries. The Chinese attack was to him a betrayal of trust and a personal defeat and humiliation.

The confrontation with China ended disastrously for India and Nehru's foreign policy came under heavy attack. Many felt that he was a spent force. Indira sensed the change in mood. Her father was now dependant on her. She nursed him, advised him on political issues and even decided which files were to be passed on to him. She also defended his interests as best she could. Ten days before her father's death she wrote to a cousin, "The campaign against Papu is studied and well organized. Every effort is being made to fully exploit recent events to weaken, and if possible, to dislodge him...... One after the other old colleagues have gone. He is surrounded by people of such small stature, of little understanding and of no loyalty or sincerity or sense of purpose."

Jawaharlal Nehru died on 27 May 1964.

Jawaharlal Nehru died on 27 May 1964.

Priya looked at a photograph of father and daughter walking on the lawns of Teen Murti Bhavan. She liked the picture. It showed a remarkably trim Nehru and a serious Indira wearing sunglasses and holding an umbrella over her father. It looked as if she was speaking and her father was listening.

Priya thought about Indira. At forty-five she was now absolutely on her own. The Teen Murti Bhavan years were over. Indira's father and husband were dead but she had discovered her passion for politics. Would she manage to outwit and outmanoeuvre the older, power hungry, conservative Congress politicians? Would she be able to carry on the work started by her father and keep his grand vision of a forward looking, democratic India alive? The task was a challenging and formidable one— did she want it? wondered Priya.

"TO BE KING IS WITHIN THE SITUATION & WITHIN ME"

YESTERDAY'S trip to Teen Murti Bhavan was a good idea," said grandfather approvingly as he put aside the newspaper he had been reading and settled the blanket on his feet. Priya and her grandparents were sitting in their small back garden, soaking in the mild afternoon sun. "You should go next to 1, Safdarjung Road. That's the bungalow Indira moved into after her father's death, and where she lived until she was assassinated in 1984."

Grandmother looked up from her knitting. "The project on Indira seems to be progressing quite nicely, Priya. Have you reached 1966—the year Mrs Gandhi became prime minister?"

"I wish I could work that fast," sighed Priya. Then a thought struck her, "Dadi, weren't you in Delhi in 1966? Tell me, what was it like then?"

"Yes," replied Priya's grandmother. She vividly remembered the month of January 1966 when Indira defeated Morarji Desai by a large number of votes to become the nation's third prime minister. On hearing the news the crowds which had gathered outside the parliament building broke into loud shouts of "Indira Gandhi Zindabad" and "Lal Gulab Zindabad". Security guards had to clear a path for Indira. Covered with garlands and sporting a red rose on her shawl she walked through the cheering masses. People saw their beloved Nehru in her, and were willing to transfer to the daughter the love and affection they had shown him.

Grandmother's mind went back to those days of 1964 when after Nehru's death Indira, overcome by grief and sorrow, had briefly thought of retiring from politics and devoting herself to setting up a memorial trust for her father. But she soon realized how unrealistic such thoughts were—politics meant too much to her for she had been attracted by its challenges. Also what better

Lal Bahadur Shastri

tribute could she pay to her father than to remain active in politics. Indira used to say that she felt her father's presence around her and she prayed that it would always be with her.

Nehru's successor, Lal Bahadur Shastri, asked her to join his cabinet arguing that her presence would bring stability to his government. Indira accepted, becoming Minister for Information and Broadcasting. By now she had moved to 1, Safdarjung Road where she continued the tradition of 'open house' started by her father. In order to remain in touch with the people she set aside an hour every morning for them. Indira kept in the public eye. As minister she made a number of important visits abroad and was outspoken on various national issues. During the two and a half years in Shastri's cabinet Indira remained firmly on the political scene. In August 1965 she was holidaying in Kashmir when Pakistani forces invaded the valley. Indira stayed on, determined to help at a time of crisis. In difficult moments her leadership qualities always came to the fore.

1965 War

The war soon ended with a peace agreement signed at Tashkent where tragically Shastri died of a heart attack.

He had successfully steered the country through the war and everybody was expecting him to continue his term in office. No one was prepared for this new turn of events.

But it did not cripple the government for too long. Soon senior Congress leaders were jockeying for power as they staked their claim to be the next prime minister. An influential group in the party wrongly thought that Indira with her reserved, uncommunicative nature would be easy to manipulate while they pulled the strings in the background. This group decided to nominate Indira as their candidate for prime minister and she accepted. She saw this as her chance. Her moment had come and she was willing and ready to seize the opportunity. But unlike the other candidates she did not reveal her ambitions, thus misleading her so-called 'supporters' into believing that she would play ball with them by remaining a figurehead. The tactics paid off, for when the votes were counted it was found that she had defeated Morarji Desai to emerge as the clear winner. She revealed her actual state of mind with lines from a poem by Robert Frost which she quoted in a letter to Rajiv, "How hard it is to keep from being king/When it is in you and the situation."

War with China and Pakistan and two prime ministers all in a period of three years—was obviously for India a very difficult and trying time.

The country was also ravaged by drought, famine, food shortage and rising prices. There was unrest on many other fronts. Rice almost disappeared from the shops, kerosene prices shot up and everyday there were demonstrations and strikes.

Amidst this Indira took office. It was an unenviable job. In the first few months as prime minister she was given a rough ride by both her party and the opposition, a situation made worse by her inexperience as decision maker. She had so far been a silent operator from behind. At Congress party meetings and in the parliament, discussions on the serious problems facing the country often broke up into chaotic, noisy scenes which she was unable to control. Nor was she able to silence her opponents with quick and decisive arguments. Ram Manohar Lohia, a senior politician at that time, sarcastically labelled her 'goongi goodiya' or 'dumb doll'.

But she learnt fast. She tried to keep her speeches as simple as possible, avoiding complicated philosophical ideas and concentrating instead on people's daily problems. She taught herself to speak and argue in a calm, dignified and confident fashion but to turn fiery if necessary. With time she became a crowd puller, building a relationship with the masses who came in thousands to see her and listen to her. She referred to them as her family, whom she had to look after like a mother. At the same time she tried to break loose from party politics and distance herself from the Congress machinery.

In the 1967 general elections she campaigned furiously travelling the length and breadth of the country and drawing huge crowds wherever she went. There were hostile scenes also. At one meeting she was hit by a stone but went on speaking with a broken, bloody nose.

Green Revolution

These elections took place against a continuing background of drought and famine and voters used the opportunity to punish the Congress for their miseries. However Indira won from her constituency of Rae Bareilly with a comfortable margin although other established Congress politicians lost their seats. Her opponents in the party clearly saw that she was a vote-catcher. So while the Congress barely won a majority in the parliament, Indira had strengthened her own position in the party. She was re-elected its leader and for a second time was asked to form a government as the prime minister. Once again she had survived the power struggle within the party and with a combination of shrewdness and fighting spirit held on to the prime minister's job.

Her initial inexperience and the tiring campaign for re- election did not deter Indira in her determination to face the country's problems. A comment she made at that time, "India simply cannot fail" could very well be true of her. The country, cost what it may, would have to pull through. "Her resolve and the attitude of getting the job done was admirable," reflected Priya's grandfather.

As prime minister her first priority was to tackle the shortage of food in the country. The situation was

"A plan to make India self-sufficient in food ...."

desperate and India was in need of food aid from abroad. Indira was forced to ask for it—an act that she considered deeply humiliating, for the aid came from the West but with conditions attached to it. After this bitter experience at the hands of aid givers she is said to have vowed never to allow herself to be put into such a situation again.

A plan to make India self-sufficient in food had already existed before Indira came to power. But she pushed it through with determination. Farmers were helped with loans to buy agricultural machines. They were given high-yielding seeds and fertilizers and their dependence on the monsoons was reduced by various irrigation projects.

"Indeed, it is because she declared war on the agricultural front that the Green Revolution gained momentum," said Priya's grandmother.

"Were there other decisions that she took?" asked Priya.

"Oh ! Indira introduced some fundamental changes which were very popular with the people." Grandmother then went on to explain that along with agriculture the financial sector engaged Indira's attention. In 1968 she started with the banks. Banks existed all over the country, some small some big, some owned by foreigners but mostly by Indians. Indira got the parliament to pass legislation to take over the largest of these from private hands and put them under government ownership, as part of her plan to tackle India's economic problems. Indira argued that the monopoly of a few powerful banking houses on the economy was harmful to the country. Through nationalization she broke this control and brought money and banking facilities to farmers in villages and also to small businesses in cities.

"And she didn't stop at that," added grandfather approvingly. "Her next move was to abolish the privy purses of the princes." Priya had read about privy purses, how at the time of independence, the Constitution allowed certain privileges to the rulers of the former princely states and also granted them and their heirs an annual sum of money for their own maintenance. In a poor country like India it was unjust that a small group of people should have such advantages forever. Accordingly, when in 1968 Indira introduced a bill in the parliament to have the Constitution amended on this point, although many princes and politicians opposed her, massive support came from ordinary people.

Priya's grandmother reminded her grandfather that between these two radical steps—bank nationalization and the abolition of privy purses—there was another event of equal significance which too marked a break with the past.

"What was it?" asked Priya inquisitively.

"The break up of the Congress party," said Grandmother. Signs of a deep rift had been obvious for some time. But matters came to a head when President Zakir Hussain died in 1967. There was a difference of opinion between Indira and others as to who should be the party's nominee for presidentship. Over the years Indira had alienated many of the established, senior members of the party with her radical views. The group that nominated her for the post of prime minister in 1966 had soon enough realized that Indira would not allow herself to be controlled by them. On her part, Indira had by then created a larger support base for herself. She had established her position, especially among the people. But she also knew that she could not afford too much quarrel within the Congress party if she was to remain prime minister and carry on her programme of changes.

Both sides tried to maintain an uneasy peace until in 1969 the arrangement broke down altogether over the issue of who should be the country's president. The Congress leadership tried to immobilise Indira by expelling her from the party. Anticipating such a move she forced the members to take sides, and the majority opted for her. The nearly hundred-year old Congress party split up. Nehru had often put party unity above his own opinions but Indira was far more practical and ruthless by nature. As both sides staked their claim to be the authentic Congress, Indira's party took the name Congress (R) and the other side was called Congress (O).

The split resulted in her gaining full control over her party. But she wanted more. She felt that her position as prime minister would be more secure if she held fresh elections and got the people's approval for the changes she had in mind. And so began the 'Garibi Hatao'—abolish poverty—campaign for the 1971 elections. These elections, according to Priya's grandmother, opened a period that would see Indira reaching great heights.

THE LEADER

P RIYA sat on her bed and spread a pile of old newspapers around her. They were more than thirty years old and yellow with age and crumbling at the edges. She glanced at the big, bold headlines announcing Indira Gandhi's dramatic decision to dissolve the parliament in December 1970 and call for early general elections in March 1971.

As Priya looked through the front page articles she gathered that at that time there was much speculation as to why Indira had taken such a decision. After the split in the Congress party, Indira could continue as prime minister only with the help of smaller political parties. Many were of the opinion that she felt her own position would be stronger and that she could get on with her programme far more easily if she had a clear backing of the people. Hence her decision to go to the polls, and see if voters approved of her policies by returning her to power with an overwhelming majority.

Indira herself said, "We are concerned not merely with remaining in power, but with using that power to ensure a better life for the vast majority of our people....The millions who demand food, shelter and jobs are pressing for action. Power in a democracy resides with the people. That is why we have decided to go to our people and to seek a fresh mandate from them."

While the opposition grouped together under the banner of "Indira Hatao" (Remove Indira), Indira hit the campaign trail with her slogan "Garibi Hatao"—Remove Poverty. She decided to appeal to the country's poor, particularly those in the villages, by focusing on their needs and promising to improve their lives. Priya looked at the faded photographs of Indira speaking at election rallies—her sari draped over her head, a garland around her neck and a sea of faces in front of her.

It was a campaign that gripped the ordinary people who turned out in thousands to listen to her and lined the roads to catch a glimpse of her. Indira responded,

projecting herself as a friend and one willing to fight for their cause. For two months she worked tirelessly from early morning until late at night, covering the entire country by air, road and rail and addressing more than four hundred meetings. Her massive effort was amply rewarded when the results started trickling in.

Priya read about the jubilant scenes at the prime minister's house as Indira received the news that she had won a two-thirds majority in the Lok Sabha. Cars went in and out of the compound, the family pets wandered in between the host of well-wishers, and flowers and sweets piled up everywhere. The normally reserved Indira shared her moment of triumph that night with her family and the crowds, saying, "I knew the people of India, who understand me, would not fail me."

At the same time as Indira was swept into power for a third term as prime minister, events of an equally dramatic nature were unfolding across the border in Pakistan.

In the general elections of December 1970, Zulfikar Ali Bhutto had emerged as the leader of the largest party in the western provinces of Pakistan. But in East Pakistan which was entirely Bengali-speaking, almost all the seats had gone to Mujibur Rahman's party. Since East Pakistan had a larger population and therefore a larger number of seats in the parliament which was being elected to draw up a constitution for the whole of Pakistan, Mujibur Rahman looked like becoming not only the prime minister of Pakistan but also its constitution maker. This created a crisis in West Pakistan, both for Bhutto who did not want to become a junior partner and for the Punjabi-dominated army that feared losing power under the new constitution.

The rest of the story can be told in Indira's own simple words in reply to a letter written by a young boy in the United States, asking the prime minister about her views on developments in Pakistan that eventually led to the civil war. "The facts about Bangladesh are quite simple," Indira wrote, "Bangladesh used to be called East Pakistan and was a province of Pakistan. But the government of Pakistan did not look after the people or pay heed to their demands regarding their language and culture and political rights. The people were very unhappy. During their elections, they voted overwhelmingly for Sheikh Mujibur Rahman but president Yahya Khan of Pakistan did not allow Sheikh Mujibur Rahman to become prime minister. Instead the Pakistan army was sent to suppress the people. Nearly three million people were killed in less than 9 months. Nearly 10 million crossed the border into India and we had to look after them."

Events in Pakistan brought to a halt Indira's election promise to the poor. Throughout 1971 she was preoccupied with the handling of the crisis in India's

With General Sam Manekshaw, Admiral Nanda and Air Marshall P C Lall.

Bengali refugees in East Pakistan crossing over to India, 1971.

backyard. As the Pakistani army bore down on the Bengalis in East Pakistan and refugees poured across the border into West Bengal, many in India demanded immediate military intervention to stop the atrocities. Indira resisted both the pressure in the country and the temptation to go to war. She was fully aware that a wrong step at that time would have resulted in accusations from abroad of war-mongering and violation of international law. Instead she maintained her calm and, as always, chose to wait for the right moment.

As she skilfully juggled with the options available to her, instant retaliation against Pakistan or building an international diplomatic pressure to make Pakistan see the light of reason, Indira quietly prepared for war so that she might not be taken unawares as her father had been, in the conflict with China in 1962. Her strategy was worked out in close co-operation with the Indian armed forces under the command of Sam Manekshaw who later became India's first Field Marshal. She competently co-ordinated her political moves with the military planners.

Months after the war, commenting on her relationship to the armed forces she said, "It was a decisive military victory, there is no doubt about that. But, what I am most proud of—not for me but for the army—is that it was so neatly done. In large part this was due to the leadership in the army and to the excellent rapport between me and the armed forces. I kept in constant touch with them."

By summer 1971 it became clear to Indira that India's important neighbour China and also the western powers were not prepared to put pressure on Pakistan to find a solution to its internal problem. Instead their opinion seemed to be that the Indian view was exaggerated and the Indians were taking advantage of the situation in East Pakistan.

So in October Indira set off on a whirlwind tour of Europe and the United States, but not before she had negotiated a friendship and co-operation treaty with the then Soviet Union. India's lonely position had pushed the prime minister to seek an alliance with the only big power that shared India's concerns, and with the signing of the treaty she knew that India could count on Soviet assistance should it be attacked.

In Europe and the United States the results of her efforts were less promising. In direct talks, Indira tried to tell the European leaders that the suffering of the people of East Pakistan had to be brought to an end and that the situation in the sub-continent could at any moment get out of control. "I am sitting on top of a volcano and honestly do not know when it is going to erupt," she said in London.

Although the Europeans showed more sympathy than the Americans, they asked India not to use military force to settle the crisis but to enter into negotiations with Pakistan. None of them was willing to tackle the basic problem of the civil war in Pakistan and the resulting atrocities on the Bengali population.

In a BBC interview at that time, Indira hit out at the silence of the western world, "There has been the worst possible violence. When Hitler was on the rampage, did you keep quiet—let Jews die? How do you control an exodus? If the world community had awoken to the situation, would it not have stopped?"

Indira's trip to the United States was even less successful.

The huge human tragedy, East Pakistan.

Priya stopped writing and picked up the photographs of the prime minister with the then American president, Richard Nixon. Both leaders looked stiff and strained and the atmosphere seemed decidedly icy. "A dialogue of the deaf" was how one newspaper described the meeting.

Indira had travelled to the United States hoping for some understanding from the government of the world's most powerful democracy. Instead she found Nixon very much on the side of General Yahya Khan, the military leader of Pakistan. Nixon was unconcerned about the violation of human rights and the huge human tragedy taking place in East Pakistan. Indira returned empty-handed but with the feeling that she had done her best to find a political solution.

The prime minister was fully aware that it was in India's interests to bring the crisis to an end. A long-running conflict on the country's borders with the

With the American president, Richard Nixon and his wife.

possibility of world powers fighting a proxy war in the region had to be stopped. Her sense of timing told her that the moment to take decisive action had come.

General Manekshaw

Priya remembered her grandparents talking about how the war began. On the night of 3 December 1971, the Pakistani air force had attacked Indian airfields. Indira was in Kolkata at that time and returned to Delhi escorted by jet fighters. She met the cabinet and the opposition leaders and on 4 December in a broadcast to the nation told the people that the country was at war. The Indian army helped by the Bengali guerilla fighters—the Mukti Bahini—entered East Pakistan and began the march to Dhaka. The United States responded by cutting off all military and economic aid to India, but not to Pakistan.

As Priya read through the old newspapers she got a sense of the enormous public support for Indira at that time. Indira herself radiated optimism and confidence and lifted the morale of both the people and the armed forces.

Throughout the campaign the head of the army, General Manekshaw, would report to her every morning. On the sixth day of the war, things were not going so well and the general was somewhat disheartened. Indira asked him about troop movements and then said calmly, "But Sam, you can't win every day." General Manekshaw was to say later, "Her courage was an inspiration."

On 6 December, Indira announced in the parliament that India recognized the new state of Bangladesh. By this time the Indian troops, supported by the navy and air force, had successfully held off the Pakistani challenge on the western front and in the east, advanced deep into Bangladesh. The quick progress of the Indian forces had by now alarmed the international community. As the United Nations Security Council debated the issue Nixon, in a show of support to Pakistan, ordered the U.S. Seventh Fleet to move towards the Bay of Bengal.

Priya had often heard her grandparents talk about Indira's forceful speech at a rally in Delhi on 12 December. Referring to the advancing American fleet, a defiant Indira told cheering crowds, "We will not retreat. Not by a single step will we move back."

On 16 December when 93,000 Pakistani officers and soldiers surrendered to Lt. General Jagjit Singh Arora in Dhaka.

With *Bangabandhu* Sheikh Mujibur Rahman after the formation
of Bangladesh.

Events were moving rapidly and Indira knew that
time was of the essence. She pushed for the takeover of
Dhaka before the American ships entered Indian waters.
The war was over on 16 December when 93,000 Pakistani
officers and soldiers surrendered to Lt. General Jagjit
Singh Arora in Dhaka. A little later on the same day, Indira
announced to a jubilant parliament that "Dhaka is now
the free capital of a free country...."

Even in the hour of her greatest triumph Indira
remained clear-headed and in control of the situation.
There was a lot of pressure on her from many in the
country that the Indian army should continue their
successful action and go into Pakistan to "teach them a
lesson." But she was wise enough to realize that such a
move though popular, would have been dangerous and

would have damaged India's standing in the world.

Above all, Indira was convinced that a democratic Pakistan was in India's best interests. Indira hoped for a situation where the Pakistani army would hand over power to a civilian government—and thus she could give democracy a helping hand. In fact, she felt that much had been done by outside powers to strengthen Pakistan's army but nothing to strengthen her people.

So on 17 December she made a statement in the parliament while announcing a unilateral ceasefire, "We should like to fashion our relations with the people of Pakistan on the basis of friendship and understanding. Let them live as masters in their own house and devote their energies to the removal of poverty and inequalities in their country. It is this sincere desire which prompted us to instruct our army, navy and air force to cease operation... on all fronts in the west." When she spoke the west was where fighting was still going on.

It was in the same spirit that she entered into an agreement with the Pakistani prime minister Zulfikar Ali Bhutto at Shimla in 1972. Her political instincts told her that there could be no lasting peace if the victor imposed his will on the defeated enemy. So she handed back most of the 5000 square miles of occupied Pakistani territory and agreed to return the 93,000 Pakistani prisoners of war once they had been cleared by the Bangladesh government.

Priya's parents had told her what they could remember about the fourteen day war. Both were in their teens at that time and described how life continued normally during the day. At night however, when the sirens howled through the darkness it got rather scary

Then they would hurriedly switch off the lights and continue doing their homework by candlelight.

But what Priya's mother remembered distinctly was the Republic Day celebrations on 26 January 1972. It was a sunny day with clear blue skies. There was unbelievable excitement and gaiety in the air. She said she had never seen such colourful tableaux, such spirited folk dances and such a smart march past as in that year.

With M.F. Husain, one of India's most well-known painters.

The Bangladesh war brought out the very best in Indira her sense of timing; her qualities of leadership and ability to take decisive action; her capacity to do several things at once; as well as her grasp of international politics. In a conversation a few weeks after the end of the war she said, "I listened, saw all the facts and a solution emerged. I then examined the solution in the harsh light of reality."

Indira was at the height of her popularity and power and some adoring supporters even compared her to the Goddess Durga. But would she be as courageous at home? Would she be able to solve the problems of poverty, hunger, unemployment and religious tension? She may have sensed the thorny path ahead of her when she said to a friend at that time, "Will we win the peace?"

HER DARKEST HOUR

P RIYA stood at the window and gazed across at the small rain-washed park in front of her house. The playground swings swayed to and fro as gusts of rain beat down on them, and there were huge puddles on the strip of flattened grass where the boys played cricket. Not a soul was in sight and even the stray dogs had sought shelter from the unpleasant weather. It was an afternoon to stay indoors. Priya sighed. The brief spell of sunny days was over and winter seemed to have returned with fresh force. She curled up in an easy chair and decided to continue reading about Indira Gandhi and events that took place nearly thirty years ago in the summer of 1975.

Meanwhile the rain continued to hammer furiously against the window panes and as Priya slowly turned over the pages of her book, her mood became as sombre as the weather outside. She was reading Indira's broadcast to the nation on 26 June 1975, with the announcement that, "The president has proclaimed an emergency. There is nothing to panic about." Indira's call not to panic could not take away the alarming character of the statement

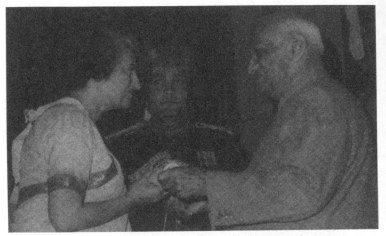

"An admiring nation awarded her its highest honour —
the Bharat Ratna."

which was to mark the beginning of the darkest hour in
her political career and a period of deep fear and
discontent in the country.

Until then it had all seemed so promising. The
Bangladesh crisis had ended successfully and in the
moment of victory India's all other problems seemed to
have been forgotten. Indira's popularity had risen to
dizzying heights and an admiring nation awarded her
its highest honour—the Bharat Ratna. Once the
celebrations were over people returned to their normal
routines. They now expected Indira to turn her attention
to the country's internal problems and make good on her
election promise of 'Garibi Hatao' which the war had
pushed to the background.

India was indeed facing some serious problems.
After a few years of good monsoons and abundant food
reserves, the rains had failed in 1972 and 1973. This in
itself was serious. But for a country whose grain reserve

had been used up in feeding millions of Bangladeshi refugees, it now took on disastrous proportions. The shortage pushed the food prices up while in the drought-hit areas drinking water became scarcer than food.

At this point Priya remembered her mother talking about the constant breakdown of electricity and water supply in Delhi during those years. Her grandmother too had spoken of standing in long queues to buy wheat, rice and sugar at somewhat affordable prices at ration shops. Normal people became restless and discontented. They felt that while Indira had raised hopes of giving them a better life, in reality she had failed even to give them enough food.

The Bangladesh war had been expensive and had left India in a bad shape economically. It also led an angry American government to cut off all economic aid. The situation was worsened by dissatisfied workers taking to the streets as a wave of strikes swept through the country. 'Bandhs' and 'gheraos' became a daily affair. Railway workers stopped work as did those in steel and fertilizer plants. Indira's government used massive force to end this agitation—particularly the railway strike. Her popularity naturally took a severe plunge.

It seemed that things could not get worse, but they did. People close to Indira in her Congress party were accused of corruption on a scandalous scale. Many suspected that this was happening with Indira's knowledge and that she chose to turn a blind eye to it. Around this time a stalwart in India's independence struggle, Jayaprakash Narayan, J.P. in short, decided to use this public anger against corruption and rising prices to organize a mass movement for change.

Poverty, overpopulation, drought, food shortages, economic failures, strikes, corruption—India was going through its worst phase since independence. But Indira did not seem to have any answers or even a desire to tackle the crisis sincerely. She began to lose state elections and was met by black flags and cries of protest at election

Jayaprakash Narayan

rallies. Public opinion shifted in favour of J.P. General elections were due to be held in 1976 and Indira's chances of success began to look doubtful.

Many who had been observing the events from close quarters were still impressed by Indira's "tremendous guts and determination." They felt that she could have been a new Gandhi but that it had all somehow got lost in the process of politicking. The prime minister was perhaps a little too concerned with remaining in power and therefore tolerated mismanagement and corruption, although in the long run these paved the way to her doom.

A feeling of insecurity and mistrust had haunted Indira ever since she entered politics when her father was prime minister. She felt that others in the Congress party were always plotting against her and bent on removing her. With time this feeling of suspicion grew stronger. "She felt everyone whispering against her—something going on behind every bush, on the other side of the wall," recalled a leading politician.

As a result of such fears, Indira sought to silence opposition of any kind both within the Congress party and outside. "She cut down all the tall poppies in one way or another," was how one newspaper article put it. Not willing to listen to criticism or to advice she surrounded herself with yes men and insensitive advisers. It seemed that the only person she seriously listened to was her younger son, Sanjay.

Sanjay Gandhi was in his late twenties in 1975. In 1955, as his mother embarked on a political career and was finding less and less time for her sons, she sent them off to a boarding school. Sanjay was nine years old and his elder brother Rajiv twelve, when they arrived in Dehradun. For the next few years Indira saw them mainly during vacations. But by the end of the 1960s both brothers were back in Delhi, living with their mother in the prime minister's residence. Neither showed any interest in politics. Rajiv married and started working as an airline pilot while Sanjay decided to set up a factory to manufacture cheap small cars.

At that time, in India, the production of cars was strictly controlled and normally such a plan would not have got government approval so easily. The Maruti project however, was given both public money and land. Although Indira was never directly involved, many said that the plan was given the green signal because Sanjay was the prime minister's son. Indira, on the other hand, felt that the opposition parties in the parliament were using Sanjay's project to hit out at her. The Maruti controversy was just one of the many problems swirling around Indira in the summer of 1975.

One other controversy, developing far more dangerously, was about the earlier 1971 general elections. Indira had at that time defeated her opponent Raj Narain to claim the Rae Bareilly seat. The latter had then gone to court claiming that Indira had won by unfair means. The grounds for his case were so flimsy that nobody had taken it seriously, and the case had dragged on for years.

Now on 12 June 1975 the judge had finally delivered his verdict. He not only found Indira guilty of violating rules and procedures connected with the elections but also barred her for six years from holding any public office. Indira's opponents were delighted, for the cour orders meant that she would have to give up her position as prime minister. They took to the streets demanding her immediate resignation.

The Allahabad High Court judgement hit the country like a bombshell. As Priya looked through the old issue of the *Illustrated Weekly of India*, she saw the black and white photographs of J.P., Morarji Desai and others surrounded by large excited crowds. Priya got a sense of the charged atmosphere of that hot summer. J.P raised passions to a fever pitch by calling on people to demonstrate against the government, prevent courts and government offices from functioning and also asked the army and the police to disobey government orders. His main aim was to force Indira and her government to resign.

Faced with an open and provocative challenge to her authority, Indira reacted. "I want something done. I

Sanjay Gandhi

feel India is like a baby, and just as one should sometimes take a child and shake it, I feel we have to shake India." She was convinced that there was a plot to destroy her and a larger one to destroy the country. Indira decided not to resign but tackle her enemies head on with all possible means. It was a decision encouraged and supported by her son Sanjay, who stood by his mother at this fateful moment.

Morarji Desai and Jayaprakash Narayan.

On the morning of 26 June 1975, Indira went on air to announce that the country had been placed under a state of emergency. By that time Jayaprakash Narayan, Morarji Desai and 600 other opposition leaders had been arrested, the press put under total government control and the fundamental rights of citizens suspended.

Later, Indira justified her decision to take such severe action by saying, "The opposition had chalked out a programme of countrywide agitation, disruption...which have resulted in a grave threat to public order and damage to the economy....This kind of programme is not compatible with democracy, it is anti-national...and could not be allowed. There should be realization that even in a democracy there are limits which cannot be crossed. Violent action and senseless satyagrahas will put down the whole edifice which has been built over the years with such labour and hope."

Indira's critics insist that there were no internal threats to the country's stability nor a serious breakdown of law and order. According to them the prime minister was simply not prepared to accept the Allahabad High Court's judgement and step down from power. The Emergency, they say, was also a convenient way to avoid general elections in 1976 which Indira feared she would lose. She had failed to provide good governance and used the Emergency laws to silence protest in a ruthless fashion in order to cover up this failure.

As Priya considered the pros and cons for declaring emergency she was keen to find out what her grandparents had felt at the time. People were no doubt shocked by the announcement of emergency but there had been very little public protest. In fact, the Emergency brought welcome and visible improvements in their daily life. Government officials could be seen working regular hours; the streets looked cleaner; prices came down; and even trains started running on time. And on a national level, according to Priya's grandfather, strikes and 'gheraos' came to an end and smugglers and hoarders found themselves behind prison bars.

But as the Emergency continued, although on the surface life remained normal, below it one could sense a growing feeling of anger and frustration. Thousands were languishing in prison without trial and the press was not allowed the freedom it had earlier enjoyed. Punctual trains and garbage free neighbourhoods were no longer enough to stop people from thinking that the government and police simply could not be trusted.

Many resented Sanjay's role during the Emergency. With all opposition silenced, Indira found herself surrounded only by flatterers. It was not surprising that in such a situation the only person she could trust completely was her son. Sanjay held no elected post in government, yet during the Emergency he became the second most powerful person in the country after his mother.

As Indira's closest adviser he was her eyes and ears. Many orders with far-reaching consequences came from him. Even government programmes were sometimes based on his ideas. Amongst his favourite projects, two—family planning and slum clearance—turned out to be so highly controversial that people became suspicious of Sanjay's motives.

But the seventies were not all years of conflict and scarcity. Two developments struck Priya because of their connection to themes which had always interested her but had gained in significance over the years.

Indira loved nature—a trait she had inherited from her father and retained from her school days in Switzerland. She felt concerned about the growing damage to the environment all over the world.

Indira loved nature.

In June 1972 she travelled to Sweden in northern Europe. There, at the capital city of Stockholm, the United Nations Organization was holding a conference on Human Environment. In a remarkable speech she boldly attacked the developed countries for being the biggest culprits in ruining the environment. This needed to be pointed out because in the name of protecting the environment the rich nations would not allow the poorer nations to have industries. Indira was a strong supporter of economic development but was equally aware of the importance of maintaining the balance between the environment and development—especially for the poorer countries. At Stockholm she spoke imaginatively about the need to plant forests, preserve bio-diversity and questioned the wisdom of dams and big irrigation projects. This was at a time when environmental issues were yet to become that fashionable as they are now.

(left) Indira Gandhi Centre for Atomic Research [IGCAR], at Kalpakkam, the second largest establishment of the Department of Atomic Energy next to (right) Bhabha Atomic Research Centre, Trombay, which was established in 1971.

The second event that deeply impressed Priya was the successful underground nuclear explosion in Pokharan, Rajasthan on 18 May 1974. Indira insisted that the country's atomic energy programme was solely for peaceful purposes. The West watched sceptically but Indira assured in a speech in the parliament that India had no intention of making a nuclear bomb. There was a profound truth in what she said in the same speech. "No

Indira Gandhi at Pokharan, Rajasthan.

technology is evil in itself. It is the use that nations make which determines its character". But she also added in a warning note to the big and powerful nations of the West that India did not accept the principle of apartheid in any matter and "technology is no exception."

Like her love of nature, the enthusiasm for science came from her father. She grasped the importance of science and technology for speeding up the process of modernization. Priya felt that Indira's support for the nuclear programme was a great help to the future of the country.

But with the Emergency in 1975 these bright spots in the fields of technology and environment were bound to be overshadowed. Months passed and it began to appear that Indira would let the Emergency continue in order to remain in power. However an inexplicable development suddenly appeared as a silver lining in those dark days.

In January 1977, Indira surprised everybody by announcing elections for 21 March. She voluntarily chose to go to the polls. Possibly she did not wish to go down in history as some kind of a dictator. Or may be deep within her there was a genuine faith in democracy.

Priya got up and looked out of the window. It was still raining. Her mind was full of questions. Would Indira win the elections? Had she lost contact with the people? Would the poor in villages and towns, her most loyal supporters, punish her for neglecting them? What if she lost the elections? Would she accept defeat and step down?

THE LAST YEARS

MISS Chopra had been making enquiries about the progress of the girls' projects. Most of them were still in the process of adding the final touches to their papers. But some had submitted their assignments and with every passing week Miss Chopra would ask one of them to introduce the personality of her choice to the class. Priya listened with interest to the presentations, for they dealt with contemporary Indian women whose names and faces she had become familiar with through magazines and television. What struck her was that quite a few of them were active feminists who used their influence to draw attention to the problems of women and who demanded for them the same rights and protection that the men enjoyed.

The discussions in the class about women's rights led Priya to think about an aspect of Indira which she had not considered before. As one of the first women in the world to head a government and India's only woman prime minister, it would have been no surprise if Indira had been a determined feminist. Priya had taken it for granted that Indira particularly, since she was acutely aware of the burning social issues, would have used the power and position of her office to better the status of women in the country. It now occurred to Priya that she had not read about any such conscious attempt on Indira's part.

At home, looking through her books, Priya came across a comment by Indira on becoming prime minister for the first time in 1966. She had been asked as to how she felt as a woman in the post of prime minister. "I do not think of myself as a woman in regard to this task," she had replied. "If a woman has the necessary qualifications for whatever profession, she should be allowed to work in the profession....I am no feminist, I'm a human being. I don't think of myself as a woman when I do my job. I'm just an Indian citizen and the first servant of the country, 'desh sevika'."

Indira often insisted that she was not the typical feminist. Imitating men or aggressive confrontation between men and women was not her idea of women's liberation. She felt that women should be given every

opportunity to develop their personalities and pursue their interests. Although Indira accepted that there were still glaring social inequalities and prejudices against women which had to be dealt with, she did not tackle them as militantly as feminists generally did. Instead she believed that obstacles "had not prevented women of character to break through all barriers and prejudices."

Priya noted with interest that during her years as prime minister, Indira had never appointed women to important positions in her cabinet. And even though, women all over the country were amongst her most loyal voters, Indira did not make women's issues one of her top priorities.

Indira's mixed attitude towards women's rights was very much on her mind as Priya resumed her story from the point in 1977 when in the midst of the Emergency, she announced the surprise general elections. Political opponents were then ordered to be released but the Emergency laws continued in force.

Indira campaigned in much the same fashion as she had done in the past—tirelessly travelling through towns and villages and addressing rallies wherever she went. But times had changed. Unlike in the past, no cheering crowds greeted her. Often people simply walked away before she had even finished speaking. Her staunchest supporters—women and the poor—were not prepared to listen to her any more.

It was the speeches of her opponents that now fired the masses with enthusiasm. The opponents J.P., Morarji Desai and others, all getting on in years, had grouped together to form the Janata party. Their main aim was to

Sanjay and Maneka Gandhi.

remove Indira from power. For the first time the veteran
of so many election campaigns was unable to strike a
chord in the people. She must have sensed that all was
not going well.

The turn-out was high on the four days of voting.
Voters could not have spoken their mind more clearly
and forcefully. When the results started coming in it
became obvious that Indira and her Congress party had
suffered a crushing defeat. The latter was almost wiped
out in northern India, losing heavily to the Janata party.

Indira herself was humiliated, losing to Raj Narain,
the man who some years ago had filed a suit against her
in the Allahabad High Court. Sanjay, her son, too lost his
constituency. Jubilant crowds greeted the news of Indira
and her party's defeat with fireworks and the celebrations
went on late into the night. At the same time in the prime

minister's residence the lights went out as silence descended. Indira had probably never felt so alone.

She took full responsibility for the disaster, knowing that in rejecting her, voters were punishing her for the Emergency. In her resignation letter of 22 March she wrote, "Elections are part of the democratic process to which we are deeply committed. I have always said, and I do believe, that the winning or losing of an election is less important than the strengthening of our country and ensuring a better life for our people....Since childhood my aim has been to serve the people to the limit of my endurance. This I shall continue to do."

Stunned by her defeat Indira considered retiring from politics and settling down in a cottage in the hills. She wrote to a close friend, "My special interests have always been children, welfare, environment, wild-life, etc. I shall try and take up some such work." Friends who visited her at home would find her sitting on the veranda

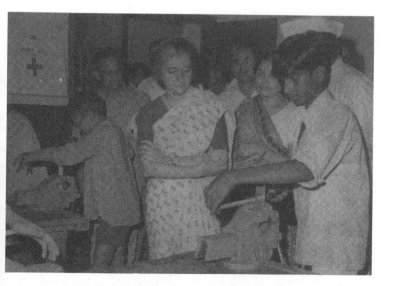

staring into the garden. But, then only sixty, Indira was really not yet ready to leave politics. She had never been one to take defeats lying down. Soon the old fighting spirit was back. She vacated the prime minister's residence and moved into another bungalow from where, within a few months, she began to take the first tentative steps back into politics.

Meanwhile one of the first acts of the Janata government was to set up a commission to look into the misdeeds of the Emergency years. Indira was more worried about Sanjay than for herself. What action would the Commission take against him?

Apart from their pursuit of Indira, the Janata government seemed to have little else on their agenda. Once the aim of defeating her had been achieved, the

union of political parties fell apart as hastily as it had been formed. Squabbling and intriguing followed amongst its leaders. Bad governance led to rising prices and a deteriorating law and order situation.

As she watched her opponents squander the enormous goodwill of the voters, Indira was quick to seize the chance. She had resumed the daily dealings with the public which used to be part of her schedule as prime minister. Now even though she was out of power, people came to tell her about their dissatisfaction with the Janata government. Over the months her earlier followers had moved away. Her former colleagues in government had ranged themselves against her and even her party had at one point advised her to keep a low profile. But now people started coming back and this gave her a new hope. Indira only hoped that they might have begun to forgive her for the excesses of the Emergency.

Priya looked at the photographs of Indira taken during these years when she was out of power. There were not many. One showed her seated on an elephant on her way to the remote little village of Belchi in Bihar where Hindu landlords had massacred a group of Harijans. This was in July 1977. It was the monsoon season, rivers had burst their banks, and due to rough weather no means of transportation—apart from the elephant—were available to take Indira to Belchi. But she was determined to go and share the misery of the survivors—just as, many years ago she had rushed to Tezpur when the Chinese had threatened Assam. She crossed the river in pouring rain and gathering darkness, and on reaching the village sat down to console the frightened Harijan women and children.

As Indira prepared for her comeback, Sanjay stayed by her side. He had now become her political partner, just when many senior members of her Congress party were turning against her. Indira, however, needed a party which she could control and with which she could contest the next elections. The stage was set for yet another split in the Congress party—the second time within ten years.

In January 1978 Indira formed a new party called the Congress(I). Her next step was to secure a seat in the parliament. At the end of 1978 there was a by-election for a Lok Sabha seat from Chikmagalur. Chikmagalur is in the coffee-growing region of Karnataka with an electorate tailor-made for Indira. Fifty per cent of the voters were women and an equally large number belonged to the Scheduled Castes.

The Janata government had hounded her over the past months giving the public the impression that harassing a lone woman was more important than governing the country. The Janata party's campaign for their candidate in the by-election was conducted in much the same style. But the image of a 'hunted' Indira did not go down well in the villages of Chikmagalur, instead it added to her popularity. Indira met the tribals and the coffee-pickers and talked to them about their daily struggles. She was welcomed as "Indira Amma" or "Mother Indira". It was hardly surprising that on the election day women in large numbers turned up to cast their votes for Indira. She won by a big majority and by the end of 1978, she was back in the parliament.

From the day Indira lost power in March 1977 she and her younger son had found themselves at the centre of many investigations and many court cases. One such investigation came to an end around the time of Indira's return to the Lok Sabha. Since Indira was found guilty of wrongdoings she was arrested and lodged for a week in Tihar jail. She also lost her seat in the parliament. It seemed very much the end of her political career. She was to comment later, "I had only two alternatives, to fight or to let them destroy me like a sitting duck."

Indira chose to fight. But she was greatly helped by the fact that the various factions within the Janata party were tearing at each other in their hunger for power. As a result the government was just stumbling from crisis to crisis. In August 1979 it finally collapsed and Sanjiva Reddy as the head of state called for general elections in 1980. Indira summed up the Janata years by saying scornfully, "They had their chance and what did they do?

They made a big mess."

An old copy of *India Today* lay buried under the pile of newspapers and magazines that Priya had collected. "Indira Heading for Victory", predicted the January 1980 issue in bold red letters on the front cover. Indira and her son had jointly charted the course of the election campaign, with the latter exercising considerable influence on his mother. She had campaigned energetically going from one dusty village to the other asking people to "elect a government that works." A government that she said would provide them with the necessities—sugar, kerosene and coal, and keep the prices of onions stable. Her Congress(I) slogan was, "Janata Party ho gai fail, kha gai chini pi gai tel,"—"Janata party has failed. It has eaten up the sugar and finished off the oil."

At election rallies Indira would raise her hand and tell the voters that that was the new symbol of her party and they were to stamp the hand symbol on their ballot

paper. The Janata hit back by reminding voters of the recent past—of the dark days of Emergency and Sanjay's controversial role in it. Democracy and civil rights would be at stake again if Indira came back to power. "Beware of the hand that comes to you open for votes today, it should not become a fist to strike at you tomorrow," they warned.

The Congress (I) slogan "Indira bulao desh bachao"—"Call Indira to save the nation" became a reality when in January 1980 she was voted into her fourth term as prime minister. Sanjay had also been forgiven for his role in the Emergency and sent to parliament from Amethi. Slowly, step by step, Indira had worked her way back to 1, Safdarjung Road.

Priya's project was now coming to an end and she wanted to have a look at the house, a silent witness to the many dramatic events in Indira's life. So she decided to ask her mother to take her there.

1, Safdarjung Road, Indira's home for nearly seventeen years was a simple white bungalow built by the British. Located at the end of Safdarjung Road where it met Akbar Road, its compound included the adjoining bungalow numbered 1, Akbar Road which was her office. The two were connected by a small gate. Priya, her mother and grandparents joined the crowd of villagers, tourists and schoolchildren all waiting to enter the former prime minister's home. Security was tight, a reminder of the dreadful event of two decades ago. The watchful eyes of stern soldiers did not allow any spontaneous movement on the part of the public. "No freedom to wander about here," complained grandfather, "better follow the signs."

Winter was finally over. It was a warm day. As they lined up at the side of the house, Priya looked around curiously. Tall old trees dotted the big garden. Blossoming bougainvillea, calendula and snapdragon provided splashes of colour amidst the green of the lawns and bushes. But the house itself looked surprisingly normal. Compared to the enormous dimensions of Teen Murti

1, Safdarjung Road

House, 1, Safdarjung Road was small and modest, but with an air of elegant simplicity. Indira had been horrified to see the house in 1980. In her years out of power the off-white walls had been repainted in shades of pink and blue and massive furniture had cluttered the rooms. She insisted on getting it all redone before she moved in.

As Priya and her family filed past the rooms, her mother pointed out the book-lined living room with its sober furniture. Priya thought she had seen a game of Scrabble lying somewhere. She remembered reading that Indira loved to play word games with her grandchildren and family. The rooms reflected Indira's impeccable taste and personal interest in decorating the house. When entertaining guests she took great care with table settings and liked the rooms to be filled with fresh flowers. On the other hand, Priya recalled having read that Indira was extremely frugal as far as her food habits were concerned. Often she would dine on a boiled potato, boiled egg and a mango or just a cutlet and vegetables.

By the summer of 1980 Indira had completed almost six months of her fourth term as prime minister. She had campaigned on a promise to tackle a number of issues which needed immediate attention—rising prices, shortages of essential items and unemployment. But she did not seem to have tackled these problems with any decisive action. There were also very serious political crises which had worsened over the months - communal tension, caste atrocities on Harijans and violent and bloody ethnic killings in Assam.

Trouble was also brewing in Punjab.

In the midst of all this, on a hot June morning, Sanjay decided to fly his two-seater plane over Delhi. As he began a series of aerial acrobatics he suddenly lost control and the plane crashed, killing both Sanjay and his co-passenger. A stunned Indira rushed to the site of the accident. At thirty-three Sanjay had all the time on his side to fulfil his political ambitions. His death was a tragic blow from which Indira never recovered.

Consoled by Rajiv at the death of Sanjay.

Yet within a few days Indira had managed to pull herself together and was back at her desk. A friend recalled asking her one evening to take some rest as she looked so exhausted. Indira replied that she still had three hours of work ahead of her that night. "Who will do this work? If I don't do it now, I will have to wake up at four in the morning."

Sanjay's death left Indira once again without a person she could trust. The problems facing her were enormous but so was her fear of potential rivals. Her sense of insecurity had only increased. She now turned to her surviving son Rajiv, hoping that he would take Sanjay's place. Rajiv was initially reluctant to join politics but was eventually persuaded to stand for the parliament from Sanjay's constituency of Amethi in June 1981. He was elected.

The crises in the country continued and Indira seemed unable and some say even unwilling to come to grips with the problems which in some cases had assumed frightening proportions. One such case was Assam.

The state had a history of tension between tribals and the plains people. There was a third element—men who had come to Assam from outside in search of a living and had settled down. The latest cause of tension was the wave of *foreigners* that had come during the Bangladesh war, when millions of refugees entered India. When the war was over, some returned but many stayed behind illegally and found jobs as cheap labour on the tea plantations of Assam. These refugees were mainly Muslims and to further complicate matters were looked upon by the Congress party as potential voters.

For a long time Indira did not act decisively, allowing the situation to drift. Now as protests and strikes brought the state to a standstill she dismissed the state government, imposed President's rule, called for fresh elections and sent in the armed forces to restore law and order.

The elections in Assam turned out to be a huge mistake and a particularly insensitive one. The immigrant issue, instead of being solved to the satisfaction of the Assamese, was seen as being exploited to further the political interests of Indira's Congress party.

In the violence that accompanied the polls that no Assamese wanted, thousands died and thousands were rendered homeless as villages burnt and Hindus, Muslims and tribals killed each other. The worst massacre took place in the small town of Nellie where many men, women and children died. Indira flew to Assam to assess the situation. "I cannot find words to describe the horrors," she said. Nevertheless Congress (I) was declared the winner of the state elections and asked to form a government.

The Assam episode made Indira increasingly insecure. She found herself unable to provide the

Massacre that took place in Nellie, a small town of Assam.

leadership needed to solve the grave internal problems. Her fine sense of timing, the ability to seize the right moment, once a powerful asset, was now missing. She gave the impression of being a tired person. A close friend described her at the time "as a woman who had run out of steam. She had always been a private person....but now she seemed to be genuinely at a loss. And more melancholic than I'd ever known her. She no longer knew whom to trust, or what advice to act on. I think she'd begun to doubt her own judgement."

Meanwhile another kind of crisis which had been simmering in Punjab for years had finally got out of control again because Indira had not taken any decisive action. It set in motion a chain of events which eventually led to her assassination.

The Punjab problem was as complicated and entangled as the one in Assam but distinctly more serious. After independence the Sikh refugees from Pakistan had settled down in East Punjab. With hard work came prosperity and the demand for a homeland of their own. But Nehru was unwilling to divide the country into states along the lines of religion. It fell to Indira to give way to the Sikh clamour for their own state and in 1966 East Punjab was divided into Punjab and Haryana.

Khalsa Symbol: demand for a separate and independent Sikh state called Khalistan

The Sikhs had got their homeland but acquiring political power proved to be more difficult. In successive elections the Akali Dal—a Sikh party—could never emerge powerful enough to govern alone in Punjab. It was forced to form alliances. Only in the state elections held after the Emergency did it win a majority. Even then it chose to form a government with the Janata party.

The alliance settled down and the Akali Dal was keen on completing its term in office. Meanwhile the Congress (I) and Sanjay, being out of power, turned their attention to destabilizing the ruling Akali Dal. The man who was brought into the picture to divide the Akali Dal was Jarnail Singh Bhindranwale.

Unfortunately for the Akalis the Janata run central government in Delhi collapsed and Indira assumed power, having won the 1980 general elections. She immediately dismissed the legally elected non-Congress state governments instead of allowing them to complete their full terms. Fresh elections were ordered. The Congress won in Punjab and the Akalis were furious. They drew up a list of Sikh grievances which included declaring Chandigarh as the exclusive capital of Punjab and a larger share of river waters for the state. As they tried to force these issues, inter-communal violence broke out. Cries for a separate and independent Sikh state called Khalistan became louder.

To make the political picture muddier Bhindranwale had in the mean-time turned against the Congress(I). He moved around with his heavily armed companions campaigning actively for Khalistan. Indira's government was criticised for doing little to control him despite his involvement in a number of violent incidents. By 1983, challenging the authority of the government, Bhindranwale and his followers had moved into the holiest Sikh shrine—the Golden Temple complex in Amritsar, and turned it into a well-protected fortress. From there they continued to spread terror.

Indira had started negotiations with the Akalis in 1981, and although the talks continued over the next two years they failed to make any headway. As the crisis in Punjab reached alarming proportions and bomb blasts and murder became routine, Indira seemed helpless. She had allowed the situation to drag on. She had also totally misjudged Bhindranwale, failing to see his criminal character and the danger he posed to India's unity. When she finally took action against him it was too late.

On the night of 30 May 1984 the army surrounded the Golden Temple complex. Operation Blue Star had begun. Over the next few days the army assessed the

Golden Temple complex. Operation Blue Star.

The last journey.

situation. On 6 June they pushed into the temple complex. The opponents were heavily armed with sophisticated weapons whereas the army had been instructed to avoid too much damage to the temple. As a result it suffered high casualties. Nevertheless damages to the temple did take place, and this angered and saddened many Sikhs. Bhindranwale was killed.

"After Operation Blue Star Indira had been receiving death threats from Sikhs but as a mark of her trust generally in the Sikh community she insisted on keeping Sikhs amongst her bodyguards," said Priya's grandmother.

It was 31 October 1984. Quite a normal day. Priya's mother vividly remembered that morning. "We went about our daily chores. Towards mid-morning we started hearing rumours that something had happened to Indira.

By afternoon it was confirmed that she had been assassinated."

For Indira the day had begun like any other day. She had taken her usual daily exercises, eaten a light breakfast, read some official papers and chatted with her grandson. Then at 9.15 she left her house to walk over to her office next door for a television interview. As she approached the gate connecting the two bungalows her Sikh bodyguards opened fire on her.

"As the news spread anti-Sikh riots broke out. Thousands of Sikhs died in tragic circumstances and lost their homes in the resulting violence. For the next few days Delhi was a very unsafe place to be in," added Priya's mother.

Priya was standing in front of the blood-splattered saffron coloured sari Indira was wearing on the day she died. Her tour of 1, Safdarjung Road had come to an end.

The cremation

She left the house and walked down the shady path to the spot where Indira lay dying that October morning. There was a plaque marking the spot where the prime minister fell. Inscribed in it were lines from her last public speech a day before she died. As Priya read the lines she was reminded of a letter Indira wrote to her father in 1944 just after the death of her uncle:

> "From the minute we are born, with that effort for breath, begins a lifetime of struggle. The years and years through infancy, childhood, manhood and old age are full of struggle, for something or the other, for health, for fame, for fortune. And then suddenly as if somebody had blown off a candle, pouff! it's all finished. The individual with his likes and dislikes, his opinions and prejudices—in fact everything that makes him what he is, is no more, is just a 'body'. And when you have lost life itself, is it any consolation that you are remembered and mourned, that you have left a big or a small mark on the world and its affairs?"

Rajiv Gandhi with the mortal remains of Indira Gandhi.

INDIRA'S LEGACY

WHEN she died at the age of 67 Indira had been in politics long enough to have become a household name. Indeed those who grew up in the years after independence and right down to the 1980s all 'knew' her in some way. Public life in India without Indira was unthinkable, such was her domination of modern India. She herself was very conscious of "living and creating history", which gave many of her actions a certain dramatic touch and she saw to it that she remained in the public eye.

Indira became prime minister at a time when the struggle for independence was over and the country had won its freedom. A different kind of leadership was needed to guide the country into the modern world and to help it take its place in the international community. Indira satisfied these requirements. Her achievements outside the field of politics are no less impressive. She was far-sighted enough to see the areas where India needed to modernize itself in order to meet the demands of a modern world. The impulses that she gave the country in the field of science and technology have had a lasting impact.

Indira was one of the few leaders who at a very early stage realised the importance of environmental protection. As prime minister she herself took charge of the departments of science and technology, space and atomic energy, clearly showing the importance she gave to these issues. Having the prime minister as their boss meant that scientists had fewer bureaucratic hurdles to deal with, and they had her ear.

She stopped work on the Silent Valley dam project in Kerala and asked for the project to be re-examined. She was aware that the use of technology in development had to be often at the expense of the environment. "Without heavy industry we cannot keep our freedom because we would be completely dependent on other countries." But as she told the scientists, "Be all the time on your toes and keep looking at the problem from all around." The two—technology and environment must be better coordinated.

New and cleaner sources of energy, such as solar energy, interested her. She also saw the necessity of keeping traditional energy-saving technology. "There is much sense in what people have evolved over the years to suit their climate, their environment, their way of living. Of course you can't keep all of it, because our way of life has changed, but I think a lot of it can be adapted and made more efficient."

Indira kept in touch with the advances in computer technology. She had heard of the chip and asked experts on computer literacy to brief her on the benefits of

Rakesh Sharma

computers for India. Indira wondered whether computers should be considered a luxury in a country where millions could not read or write. She saw it as a practical necessity. "In India I would say if a computer made a lot of difference to efficiency, you should get it. Where there is efficiency there is greater production...that makes for more employment." The next prime minister, Rajiv Gandhi, and his advisers built on the base Indira had prepared.

India's nuclear programme for peaceful purposes was a programme she pushed through despite heavy criticism from the West. That, and India's space programme both got unstinted backing from her. Indian scientists successfully launched the Rohini -1 in 1980 and in 1984 Rakesh Sharma became the first Indian in space when he joined the crew of the Soviet Salyut-7 space station.

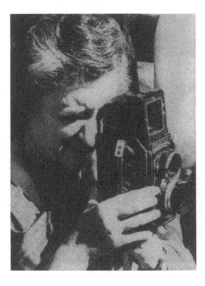

Nearly twenty years after her death, many of the issues that today influence people's lives in India can be traced back to the innovative beginnings made by Indira Gandhi.

Priya had spent the last few months reading about Indira and talking to her grandparents to get first hand impressions of her. Indira was a controversial personality and while she had many critics she also had an equally large number of admirers. But if there was one feature of Indira that stood out above all others and above all controversy, one feature which Priya wished to put across forcefully to her classmates, it was Indira's love for her country.

It was a love which manifested itself in many ways — in the manner in which Indira was able to reach out to millions of poor people; or the fierce pride with which she fought to maintain the country's dignity and independence in world forums; her effort to protect India's interests during the Bangladesh crisis; and the determination with which she tried to overcome the never ending cycles of droughts, shortages and other disasters in the early years of her term as prime minister. She simply did not want to see India fail.

As she turned to go home after the journey through 1, Safdarjung Road, Priya recalled Indira's words which she had come across in one of her books. Speaking on the floor of the Lok Sabha in 1966 Indira had said, "India simply cannot fail. We are all in this together. It is not a question of this government or that government. We simply cannot fail." Priya decided that with these words she would present to her classmates the next day at school—her portrait of Indira Gandhi.

Made in the USA
Middletown, DE
15 June 2021

42239058R00083